UNITED KINGDOM
in Pictures

VGS

Kumari Campbell

Lerner Publications Company

Contents

Lerner Publications Company
A division of Lerner Publishing Group
241 First Avenue North
Minneapolis, MN 55401 U.S.A.

Website address: www.lernerbooks.com

web enhanced @ www.vgsbooks.com

CULTURAL LIFE ······ 46

► Religion. Literature, Music, and the Arts. Theater, Television, and Film. Festivals and Holidays. Sports and Recreation. Food.

THE ECONOMY ······ 58

► Manufacturing and Trade. Transportation, Tourism, and Services. Agriculture. The Future.

FOR MORE INFORMATION

Library of Congress Cataloging-in-Publication Data

Campbell, Kumari.
    United Kingdom in pictures / by Kumari Campbell.—Rev. & expanded.
        p.   cm. — (Visual geography series)
    Includes bibliographical references and index.
    Contents: The land—History and government—The people—Cultural life—The economy.
    ISBN: 0-8225-1995-X (lib. bdg. : alk. paper)
    1. Great Britain—Pictorial works. [1. Great Britain. 2. Northern Ireland.] I. Title. II. Visual geography
series (Minneapolis, Minn.)
DA667.C28 2004
941—dc22   2003016539

Manufactured in the United States of America
1 2 3 4 5 6 - BP - 09 08 07 06 05 04

INTRODUCTION

Although small in size, the United Kingdom of Great Britain and Northern Ireland (UK)—often referred to simply as Britain—has long been one of the most powerful nations in the world. At the height of its power, during the 1800s and early 1900s, Britain commanded an empire that spanned six continents and owned the world's most powerful naval fleet.

The United Kingdom of Great Britain and Northern Ireland is located in the North Atlantic Ocean, slightly to the northwest of continental Europe. England, Scotland, and Wales make up the main island of Great Britain (along with several smaller islands), while Northern Ireland covers the northeastern part of the island of Ireland.

The unity of Great Britain dates back to 1707, when the parliaments of England and Scotland merged. (Wales had already been united with England in 1536.) In 1801 Ireland's government was united with Great Britain and remained so until the division of Ireland in 1922, when the Irish Free State (later known as the Republic of Ireland) was formed. At that

time, the six northeastern counties of Ireland remained a part of the United Kingdom and were renamed Northern Ireland.

Before the first century A.D., Celtic tribes from north-central Europe settled in the area that later became the United Kingdom. This Celtic ancestry has formed the basis of the country's history, language, and culture. Being forced to defend its territory over a period of centuries against invaders such as the Romans, the Anglo-Saxons, the Vikings, and the Normans eventually strengthened Britain. From the 1500s onward, victories in several wars against European rivals allowed Britain to acquire much territory around the world. By the 1800s, Britain had become the world's most dominant colonial power.

During the nineteenth century, Britain drew on the natural resources of its colonies and the ingenuity of its people to design and build machines to perform tasks that had previously been done manually by human beings. Britain's efforts established the Industrial Revolution, a major milestone in human progress.

SHETLAND
ISLANDS

NORTH
SEA

ORKNEY
ISLANDS

NORTH
ATLANTIC
OCEAN

OUTER HEBRIDES

INNER HEBRIDES

Caledonian Canal *Great Glen*

Loch Ness

SCOTLAND

Tay R.

Loch Tay

Firth of Tay

NORTH SEA
OIL FIELDS

Loch Lomond

Clyde R.

Glasgow ● ★ Edinburgh

Firth of Clyde

Oil Pipeline

Lough Foyle

RATHLIN ISLAND

Londonderry ●

Foyle River

Lower Bann R.

North Channel

Hadrian's Wall

ENGLAND

Belfast ★

Lough Neagh

Upper Bann R.

Lagan

Ouse River

NORTHERN
IRELAND

IRISH SEA

Aire River

Bradford ● Hull ●

Leeds ●
Manchester ●

Liverpool Bay

Liverpool ●

Gas Pipeline

REPUBLIC
OF
IRELAND

Dee R.

Trent River

Cardigan Bay

Birmingham ●

Stilton ●

Severn River

WALES

Milford Haven ●

London ★

Cardiff ★

Thames River

Bristol ●
Cheddar ●

Bristol Channel

White Cliffs
of Dover

Dover ●

Southampton ●

Channel Tunnel

Sangatte ●

English Channel

FRANCE

In the 1900s, when the United Kingdom was at the height of its power, it experienced two devastating world wars and subsequent changes in world economies, markets, and trading practices. These events toppled the modern United Kingdom from its pinnacle among the developed nations of the world.

In the twenty-first century, the country faces a number of challenges. It continues to balance the unique and different needs of the four independently governed political entities that make up the country. Its financial resources have been stretched to care for its citizens' needs from birth to death. The kingdom has also felt the impact of a diverse population that is increasingly made up of immigrants from former colonies with differing religious and ethnic backgrounds.

Perhaps Britain's greatest challenge will be learning to live comfortably as a member of the European Union (EU), a growing organization of European states created to foster cooperation among members. As a nation that has governed itself independently for centuries, the United Kingdom is gradually getting used to living within an economic union of many European nations, in which many economic and social decisions are made outside its own territory. Britain's population is clearly divided on the issue of European integration, and debate over the extent of the country's involvement with its continental neighbors continues.

Following the September 11, 2001, terrorist attacks on the United States, British prime minister Tony Blair pledged the United Kingdom's support to the United States in its war on international terrorism. Since that time, Great Britain has been a key ally in the United States' hunt for al-Qaeda, the terrorist group based in the South Asian nation of Afghanistan that was believed to have been responsible for the September 11 attacks. British forces participated in the U.S.-led invasion of Afghanistan in late 2001, destroying al-Qaeda's bases and the government that supported them.

In 2003 British forces once again fought alongside the United States, this time in the Middle Eastern nation of Iraq. The United States, Britain, and several other countries formed a coalition (group) to topple the regime (rule) of Iraqi leader Saddam Hussein, whom Blair and U.S. president George W. Bush believed was harboring illegal weapons and possibly selling such weapons to terrorists. After a six-week war, coalition forces had destroyed Saddam's rule and begun the process of helping Iraq to rebuild itself as a democratic state. In 2004 British forces remain in Iraq working toward this end.

THE LAND

The official name the United Kingdom of Great Britain and Northern Ireland refers to four individual countries that form a single nation. England, Scotland, and Wales occupy the island of Great Britain, while Northern Ireland is made up of six northeastern counties on the island of Ireland.

Topography

The UK takes up most of the landmass known as the British Isles (the island of Great Britain, the island of Ireland, and many other smaller islands). The British Isles lie in the North Atlantic Ocean, northwest of mainland Europe. The UK is separated from continental Europe by the English Channel (to the south) and the North Sea (to the east). The Irish Sea separates England from Ireland, while the North Channel lies between Scotland and Northern Ireland. In total land area, the UK covers 94,214 square miles (244,014 square kilometers), which is slightly smaller than the state of Oregon.

web enhanced @ www.vgsbooks.com

England occupies most of the island of Great Britain, covering an area of 50,333 square miles (130,362 sq. km). It is slightly larger than the state of New York. One of the main topographical features of England is its deeply indented coastline, which has given the country many natural deepwater harbors. In northern England, the Pennine Chain of uplands (highlands) runs in a north-south direction between the Scottish border and the middle of the country. Fertile plains lie on either side of the worn-down Pennines.

South of the Pennines, river valleys and gently rolling hills cover most of southern England. The country's most fertile agricultural land lies within the area of central England known as the English Lowlands. Most of England's population lives in this region. The east-ernmost part of this area is referred to as the Fens, an old English word meaning "marsh." The western half of southern England is dotted with moors—infertile tracts of grasses and shrubs. In the southeastern corner of England, the soil has a very high chalk content. The valleys,

SHETLAND
ISLANDS

ORKNEY
ISLANDS

NORTH
SEA

NORTH
ATLANTIC
OCEAN

OUTER HEBRIDES

NORTHWEST
HIGHLANDS

Cromarty Firth

SCOTLAND

Loch Ness

HIGHLANDS

Caledonian Canal

Great Glen

INNER HEBRIDES

GRAMPIAN MOUNTAINS

Ben Nevis

Tay R.

Loch
Tay

Firth of Tay

NORTH SEA
OIL FIELDS

Loch
Lomond

Clyde R.

CENTRAL
LOWLANDS

Firth of Clyde

SOUTHERN
UPLANDS

CHEVIOT HILLS

Oil Pipeline

Lough
Foyle

RATHLIN
ISLAND

Foyle
River

SPERRIN
MTNS.

Lower
Bann R.

ANTRIM
HILLS

North Channel

PENNINE CHAIN

Ouse River

Aire River

Lough
Neagh

Lagan R.

Upper
Bann R.

MOURNE
MTNS.

Trent River

Gas Pipeline

NORTHERN
IRELAND

IRISH SEA

Liverpool
Bay

Mount
Snowdon

THE FENS

REPUBLIC
OF
IRELAND

Dee R.

ENGLAND

Cardigan
Bay

CAMBRIAN
MTNS.

Severn River

WALES

COTSWOLD HILLS

Thames River

Bristol Channel

ENGLISH LOWLANDS

White Cliffs
of Dover

English Channel

United Kingdom

Feet	Meters	
9843	3000	Mountains
6582	2000	Uplands
3281	1000	
1640	500	Lowlands

Elevation

N

International border

Country border

Canal

▲ Mountain peak

0   100 Miles

0   100 KM

FRANCE

or downs, are mainly covered by grasses, while the tall cliffs end abruptly at the ocean in a spectacular display of chalky white soil.

Scotland covers 30,414 square miles (78,772 sq. km), an area similar in size to the state of South Carolina. The mainland of Scotland is divided into three main geographical regions, all of which lie in a northeastern-southwestern orientation. To the north is the mountainous region called the Highlands, which is divided by the Great Glen (a narrow, deep valley) into the Northwest Highlands and the Grampian Mountains. The Highlands, which rise to elevations of over 3,000 feet (914 meters), cover two-thirds of Scotland and are sparsely populated. The tallest peak in the range is Ben Nevis, which, at 4,406 feet (1,343 m), is the tallest in the United Kingdom.

South of the Highlands are the Central Lowlands, a narrow valley that is home to three-quarters of Scotland's population. Scotland's two largest cities—Edinburgh and Glasgow—are located in this region.

Bounding the lowlands on the south side are the Southern Uplands. Though mountainous, they are not nearly as high or craggy as the Highlands. Largely made up of moors, the Southern Uplands provide grazing land for sheep and cattle.

In addition to the mainland, Scottish territory also includes three groups of islands—the Shetlands, the Orkneys, and the Inner and Outer Hebrides. Most of the islands' residents raise livestock or crops.

The bleak and barren **Highlands** region covers most of northern Scotland.

Mount Snowdon is a 3,560-foot (1,068-meter) peak nestled in northern Wales. It is a popular destination for mountain climbers

Wales occupies a peninsula in southwestern Great Britain covering 8,019 square miles (20,768 sq. km), an area about the size of Massachusetts. To the east, Wales shares a land border with England. Liverpool Bay, the Bristol Channel, and Cardigan Bay lie to the north, south, and west, respectively. The Cambrian Mountains cover two-thirds of the landmass of Wales. Most of the population lives in the low-lying coastal regions and in the fertile river valleys, both of which support crop and livestock farming.

Made up of six of the nine counties that originally formed the ancient Ulster region of Ireland, Northern Ireland also includes Rathlin Island and several tiny islands in the North Channel. Northern Ireland covers an area of 5,452 square miles (14,120 sq. km) and is approximately the size of the state of Connecticut.

Most of Northern Ireland consists of low, flat, marshy plains that have been drained and converted into fertile farmland. Low mountains are scattered throughout the country, but the three primary mountain regions are the Sperrin Mountains in the northwest, the Antrim Hills in the northeast, and the Mourne Mountains in the extreme southeast. Most of Northern Ireland's land is used for crop farming and grazing.

Rivers and Lakes

England has no large lakes but has many rivers. These waterways have formed important harbors at their estuaries (points at which they flow into the ocean). Chief among these rivers is the Thames River, on whose banks rests the capital city of London. Emerging from the Cotswold Hills in the west, the river flows 215 miles (346 km) eastward to drain into the North Sea. The 220-mile (354-km) Severn River is England's longest waterway. It begins in Wales and flows eastward into England, then curves southwestward to empty into the Bristol Channel. The country's third-longest river, the Trent, begins in the middle of England and follows a U-shaped curve to join with the Aire and Ouse Rivers, which flow down from the Pennines.

Scotland's longest river, the Tay, flows from its source in the Grampian Mountains 120 miles (193 km) eastward to the Firth (bay) of Tay on the North Sea. Along the way it forms Loch (lake) Tay. Scotland's busiest waterway, the Clyde, has its source in the Southern Uplands and flows northwestward to the Firth of Clyde on the North Channel.

Scotland has many lakes, the largest of which is Loch Lomond, located in the Central Lowlands. Loch Ness, one of the deepest, lies in the Great Glen. These lakes have been connected by a series of canals known as the Caledonian Canal, which forms a continuous 60-mile (97-km) waterway between the North Sea and the North Channel.

NESSIE

The mythical Loch Ness Monster (referred to as Nessie) has lured thousands of tourists to Loch Ness (*below*) since the publication in 1934 of a photo of something resembling a long-necked creature in the middle of the lake. Many studies and searches of the lake have been conducted over the years, with no proof of such a creature. Yet many people still believe Nessie exists.

The Dee, Wales's primary river, flows eastward from the Cambrian Mountains north to Liverpool Bay. Northern Ireland has a number of important rivers, including the Upper Bann and the Lower Bann. Both travel through Lough (lake) Neagh to reach the North Channel. The Foyle, which forms part of Northern Ireland's western boundary with the Republic of Ireland, eventually empties into Lough Foyle. Lough Neagh, which covers an area of 153 square miles (396 sq. km), is the largest inland body of water in the British Isles.

Climate

The United Kingdom has a mild climate influenced by the Gulf Stream, a warm ocean current that flows from the Gulf of Mexico across the Atlantic Ocean. The moist Gulf Stream not only creates moderate temperatures throughout much of northwestern Europe, but the Gulf Stream also creates precipitation, mostly in the form of rain. Only the Scottish Highlands and the extreme northeastern areas of Scotland receive significant amounts of snow during the winter.

Average temperatures range between 40°F (4°C) in winter and 63°F (17°C) in summer for lowland and southern regions. Northern and highland regions range between 30°F (-1°C) in winter and 53°F (12°C) in summer. Average annual rainfall ranges between a low of 20 inches (51 centimeters) in the Fens and a high of 200 inches (508 cm) on the west-facing slopes of the Scottish Highlands. Average rainfall tends to range between 50 to 80 inches (127 to 203 cm) annually. October and December typically receive the most rainfall. June is generally the driest month throughout the United Kingdom.

Flora and Fauna

As a relatively small land area with a large population, the United Kingdom has experienced centuries of human settlement. As a result, its natural habitats are seriously depleted of native plant and animal life. Concern for this damage to natural habitats has caused the United Kingdom to create laws to restore and preserve the nation's forests and waterways.

Forests once covered most of the British Isles. Oak was the predominant forest species in the United Kingdom, but over the past five hundred years, most of the trees have been used for shipbuilding, fuel, housing construction, and other needs. The islands' growing population density during those centuries also required large tracts of forests to be cleared for farming, industrialization, and human habitation. By the 2000s, less than 10 percent of the country remains forested. Most of these forests consist of hardwood species such as oak, beech, ash, rowan, and birch. In northern regions, particularly Scotland, the primary forest

Highland cattle live in the Highlands of Scotland and have adapted to the rugged terrain and harsh climate of their northern location. Highland cattle have extremely shaggy, long hair to keep them warm. They also are very independent, solitary, and rather unfriendly toward humans.

vegetation is softwood, mostly pine and spruce. Some of the older and more remote Scottish forests contain Scotch pines that are more than two hundred years old.

The United Kingdom's moist, mild climate is perfectly suited for a variety of grasses, mosses, ferns, and shrubs to thrive. These cover the moors and bogs (lands saturated with water and decayed vegetation) that occupy 25 percent of the country's land.

The largest mammals in the country are red deer, abundant in the Highlands, and roe deer that thrive in all wooded regions. Carnivores such as foxes, weasels, badgers, and otters are plentiful in rural areas, as are insectivores such as moles, shrews, and hedgehogs. The European polecat, a member of the weasel family, exists only in Wales. Rabbits and brown hare thrive throughout the lowlands, while the mountain hare is native to Scotland and the Irish hare to Northern Ireland. Rodents such as rats, mice, and squirrels are also plentiful, as are toads, frogs, and other species of reptiles.

The burrowing **Eurasian badger** lives in a system of interconnected tunnels and chambers called a sett.

About 200 species of birds are found in the United Kingdom. More than half are migratory birds that only stop on their way to or from their nesting sites. Among the native species are the sparrow, blackbird, chaffinch, starling, and game birds such as pheasant, grouse, and wild pigeon. Woodpeckers, osprey, and crossbills are also common in certain areas of the country. The rugged granite cliffs of Scotland and Northern Ireland are good breeding grounds for puffins, gannets, and gulls.

Pollution and overfishing have depleted the fish stocks of many British rivers, so that they no longer provide fish as a food source. But fishing for sport is still a popular pastime. Much of the ocean fish species have also been depleted due to overfishing, but limited quantities of cod, haddock, whiting, mackerel, turbot, herring, and plaice remain.

Natural Resources

For many years, the United Kingdom's vast coal deposits were its most plentiful natural resource and the major fuel source for generating electrical power. Yet in recent decades, coal has lost its importance, following the discovery and production of oil and natural gas in the North Sea. The United Kingdom is the tenth-largest oil producer in the world. Natural gas from the North Sea is used throughout the United Kingdom to produce heat and electricity.

> **Most of the downs of southern England are made of white chalk, covered with grass, so that the chalk is not readily visible. However, where the hills meet the sea, the cliffs form white walls. British soldiers and travelers returning from Europe long to see the famous White Cliffs of Dover.**

Other mineral resources are not plentiful in the United Kingdom. Limestone, slate, sand, gravel, chalk, talc, clay, and gypsum are mined in sufficient quantities to supply the country's needs. Northern Ireland exploits its deposits of basalt, limestone, granite, sand, gravel, chalk, and peat for domestic use.

Urban Centers

With 90 percent of its population living in urban centers, the United Kingdom is considered the most urbanized country in the world. More than 30 percent of the population is clustered into seven conurbations (urban centers containing one or more large cities and towns and their

Britain's capital city, **London,** is home to some of the world's most recognizable landmarks, such as the enormous clock tower Big Ben *(center)*.

surrounding suburban and industrial districts). The Greater London conurbation contains the nation's capital city. London, population 7,285,000, is one of the world's largest and most culturally rich cities. The city is also a major tourist destination, a center for learning, and one of the world's major financial centers, with the world's largest foreign exchange and insurance markets.

London is home to Buckingham Palace, the main residence of the British royal family, and the Tower of London, an ancient fortress that houses the British crown jewels (the royal family's ceremonial jewels). The city also contains the British Parliament, where the British legislature meets, and a host of other historic buildings. In recent years, the dockyards and warehouses along the Thames River—once used by Britain's huge shipping industry—have been renovated to house modern shopping and entertainment districts.

Secondary Cities

The Midlands conurbation is centered on England's second-largest city, Birmingham (population 1,013,200), which gained its importance as a manufacturing center due to nearby coal and iron ore deposits. Birmingham factories produce cars, electronic equipment, and many other goods.

Visit vgsbooks.com where you'll find links to more information about the United Kingdom's cities—including what there is to see and do; the climate and weather; population statistics; and more.

North-central England is dominated by three major conurbations created around the cities of Leeds (726,800), Bradford (483,700), Liverpool (458,000), and Manchester (431,100). Leeds is a major cultural and educational center for northern England and supports an important wool industry. Liverpool is England's main port on the Irish Sea and manufactures cars, flour, and sugar. Manchester is an important financial center and manufactures cottons, chemicals, computers, food, tools, and electronic equipment.

Scotland's Clydeside conurbation is located in the heavily industrialized Central Lowlands. At its center, the city of Glasgow (population 668,100) is Scotland's primary shipping port. Edinburgh (population 451,700), Scotland's capital and cultural center, is also an important port and contains brewing, paper, and textiles industries.

Cardiff, the capital of Wales, has a population of 324,400 and is Wales's largest city. Located in the industrial region of southern Wales—where 75 percent of the country's population lives—Cardiff is a major port, a manufacturing center for auto parts, chemicals, electrical equipment, tobacco, beer, and steel, and an important educational and cultural center.

Shoppers and sightseers crowd Mermaid Quay, a small commercial district on Cardiff Bay in **Cardiff,** Wales's capital city.

Northern Ireland's capital, **Belfast,** has been an important port city since the twelfth century.

Belfast, with a population of 284,400, is the capital of Northern Ireland. Located on the Lagan River estuary, the city has long been a major shipbuilding center and is known for its linen, food processing, and aircraft industries. The seat of Northern Ireland's government, education, business, and cultural activities, the city has also witnessed much violence between Catholics and Protestants.

HISTORY AND GOVERNMENT

More than one million years ago, during a past ice age, the southern part of the British Isles was connected to the European mainland by a land bridge. Archaeological evidence shows that, as far back as 200,000 years ago, people from the mainland crossed the land bridge and lived in caves in southern Wales.

As the earth's climate changed between about 5000 and 6000 B.C., the melting ice submerged the land bridge, separating the British Isles from the mainland. From then until 2000 B.C., several waves of migrants are believed to have arrived by boat from the mainland.

By 2000 B.C., a new group of people from the region of present-day Germany had arrived with weapons and tools made of bronze. Evidence of these Bronze Age people has been found in all four countries of the United Kingdom. The newcomers farmed crops, raised livestock, and lived in relative peace and harmony for the next 1,500 years.

Around 500 B.C., the Celts, a people from north-central Europe, invaded the British Isles. They had developed a process of making

weapons and tools from iron. Over the next 250 years, the Celts spread throughout the islands, easily gaining control with their superior iron weapons and spreading their language, culture, and farming methods.

The Romans

In the first century B.C., the armies of Rome, an expanding empire based in Italy, landed troops in southern England to establish a colony in the British Isles. In A.D. 43, Roman troops defeated the Celts and created a new province that they called Britannia, after the Brythonic Celts who lived there. Residents of the province were known as Britons. More Romans emigrated from other parts of the empire, populating the rest of England, and building cities, roads, and forts. Romans had moved into Wales by A.D. 70, and by A.D. 80, England and Wales were completely under Roman control.

The Romans soon turned their attention to Scotland, whose Celtic population proved to be a difficult adversary. Although they were no match for the invading Roman armies and were defeated in A.D. 84, the Scottish Celts continued to invade and harass Roman settlements until the second century. To keep them out, Roman emperor Hadrian ordered the building of a fortified wall (later named Hadrian's Wall) between northern England and Scotland in A.D. 122.

The Romans ruled Britannia for the next two centuries and introduced Christianity, a religion the Romans had adopted. Christian missionaries also began to spread this faith in Ireland and Scotland. Then, in the fourth century, disputes in Rome forced the empire's rulers to concentrate their attention closer to home. By the early fifth century, the Roman Empire had begun to crumble, and its rulers abandoned many of its territories, including Britannia.

Meanwhile, in Ireland, warring Celtic chiefs had consolidated the entire island into five main territories that were controlled by the five most powerful clans (independent family groups). One of these territories was Ulster in northeastern Ireland.

◉ Foreign Invaders

As the Romans abandoned Britannia, outsiders invaded the province. Picts from the Scottish Highlands invaded northern and western Britannia. Irish Celts, known as Scotti, attacked from the west. Meanwhile, Germanic groups from northern Europe were searching for new lands to conquer. These groups, which included the Angles and Saxons, began raiding the islands, causing upheaval throughout Britannia. Many of these invaders eventually settled in the area, imposing their customs and non-Christian beliefs on the local population.

By the end of the sixth century, the Anglo-Saxons had taken over much of the island of Great Britain. The area came to be called England, from the Anglo-Saxon words meaning "Land of the Angles." During this period, Roman Catholic missionaries were sent from Rome to convert the Anglo-Saxons to Roman Catholicism. These missions were successful, and the religion took firm hold in England. Christianity also spread to the area that later became Wales, although the Celts practiced a different form of Christianity that was not controlled by Rome. They also maintained distinct language and cultural differences from the Anglo-Saxons to the east.

In the late 700s, adventurers from Scandinavia (Norway, Sweden, and Denmark) known as Vikings invaded the islands, looting coastal towns for treasure and capturing prisoners to use as slaves. After decades of conducting raids, some Vikings decided to conquer England and settle there, occupying most of the Anglo-Saxon territories. In 878 King Guthrum of Denmark waged war on Wessex (in central and

southwestern England), the last remaining Anglo-Saxon kingdom, but was defeated by King Alfred. By 886 the two kings had agreed on boundaries for their kingdoms. Guthrum would control most of northern and eastern England, and Alfred would rule much of the rest. The Danish king's lands became known as the Danelaw.

Earlier, Vikings from Norway had occupied the outlying islands and much of the coastal regions of modern Scotland. Viking raids and Scotti attacks weakened the Picts. As a result, Scotti king Kenneth MacAlpin had managed to gain power over much of northern Scotland in the mid-800s. In the following centuries, succeeding Scotti kings expanded their territories. In 1034 Duncan I came to the throne, unifying all of the Scotti lands into one kingdom, which became known as Scotland. The Vikings still held the outlying islands.

During the same period, the various Celtic kingdoms of Wales were forced to defend themselves against both Viking and Anglo-Saxon attacks. Only one king, Gruffydd ap Llwelyn, who ruled during the eleventh century, was ruthless enough to overrun all the kingdoms and bring them under his rule. But his reign was brief. To hold off invasions from England, Welsh rulers were eventually forced to swear allegiance to the Anglo-Saxon monarchy.

The Vikings also invaded and looted Ireland, conquering territory and establishing outposts. The raiders met their greatest resistance in the north, where clans joined forces to better defend themselves. By the eleventh century, all of Ireland was united under a strong leader named Brian Boru, who was proclaimed king of Ireland. In 1014 Boru and his forces faced the Vikings in a climactic battle. Boru was killed in the fight, but the Vikings were forced to withdraw.

Norman England

In 1066 English king Edward died without an heir, and his brother-in-law Harold II succeeded him. But Harold II was not a direct descendant of the royal family. A branch of Edward's family lived in Normandy, a kingdom in France. William of Normandy saw an opportunity to take over Edward's kingdom.

On October 14, 1066, the Normans defeated Harold at the Battle of Hastings. William of Normandy became King William I (the Conqueror), the first Norman king of England. He brought French-speaking Normans to England and introduced the Norman system of feudalism to the realm. Under feudalism each layer of society controlled those below it. The king controlled the nobles, who in turn controlled those who worked for them. The king and his nobles owned all the land, which was worked by powerless laborers called serfs. Serfs has little personal freedom and virtually belonged to their masters. Over the following century, feudalism took root throughout England.

Under threat of war, the powerful Normans forced the Scottish king Malcolm III to acknowledge the greater authority of Norman rule, even though the Scots kept their own kingdom. In time, heirs to

This famous tapestry shows **King Harold II (standing)** sailing to Normandy. This 1064 voyage ended in shipwreck for Harold. William of Normandy claimed that, while stranded in Normandy, Harold had promised him the English crown. But it wasn't until William defeated Harold at the Battle of Hastings that he claimed the throne.

the Scottish throne were educated in England, and so Scotland began following the government and social systems of England.

Having conquered England, William I took steps to put Wales fully under his authority. He allowed his nobles to claim Welsh lands that bordered England. Over the following two centuries, the Welsh avoided further intrusion into their domains by making alliances with the Normans, swearing oaths of loyalty, and intermarrying with them. Over the century that followed, the Normans conquered Ireland as well.

In 1154 William's grandson Henry inherited the English throne, taking the name Henry II and calling his dynasty (family of rulers) Plantagenet. Under Plantagenet rule, feudalism remained the dominant system. Most people lived and worked on the farming estates of the nobility. Because of the monarchy's holdings in both England and France, trade between the two countries expanded. In particular, English wool was a prized commodity on the European mainland.

During the first two centuries of Plantagenet reign, the country enjoyed relative security from foreign attacks but was never free from internal conflict. The monarchs quarreled with the nobility (or barons) because they thought the king held too much power. Finally, in 1215, the barons rebelled and forced Henry II's son John to sign a document called the Magna Carta (Latin for "Great Charter"), a contract protecting the rights of his subjects. Later in the thirteenth century, the barons forced King John's son Henry III to accept a parliament made up of barons, who advised him on how to govern the country.

At about the same time, the Scottish nobles also imposed a parliament on their monarch. But English attempts to seize control of the country led to decades of war between England and Scotland. The wars with England continued until 1328, when the English king Edward III finally agreed to Scotland's full independence.

The Tudors and the Stuarts

In 1337 Edward III claimed the throne of France, unleashing a series of wars known collectively as the Hundred Years' War (1337–1453). The English experienced both dramatic victories and miserable defeats. By the early 1400s, English troops had taken control of large regions of France. But by the war's end, the French had regained most of their territory. As the Hundred Years' War was drawing to a close, civil war erupted within England, as two rival families—the House of Lancaster and the House of York—fought for the throne. This war lasted for decades until 1485, when a member of the House of Lancaster, the Welsh noble Henry Tudor, defeated his opponent in the Battle of Bosworth Field. Parliament proclaimed Tudor King Henry VII.

The country prospered under Henry VII. He strengthened the economy by expanding the wool and woolen fabric trade. One of his daughters, Margaret, married the king of Scotland. The other, Mary, married the king of France. Upon his death in 1509, his son Henry VIII inherited a prosperous and stable kingdom.

Henry VIII

At that time, a movement called the Protestant Reformation was sweeping across Europe, as large numbers of people began questioning the authority of the Roman Catholic Church. Henry VIII, a devout Roman Catholic, rejected the church when the pope refused to grant him a divorce from his wife, who had failed to provide him with a male heir. Henry VIII broke all religious ties with Rome and declared himself head of the Protestant Church of England, or Anglican Church, in 1534.

In 1536 Henry VIII officially united England and Wales. English became the official language of Wales, while the Church of England became its official church. However, Henry and his successors had more difficulty introducing Protestantism to Ireland, despite proclaiming himself king of Ireland in 1541.

In 1547 Edward VI, Henry VIII's son and successor, declared Protestantism the official religion of Ireland. He took land from Irish nobles who refused to convert, giving it to English Protestants whom he had sent from England. Thus began a "plantation" system in Ireland, in which English citizens were "planted" in Ireland, displacing the native Irish.

Queen Elizabeth I came to the throne after Queen Mary I. She ruled Britain for forty-four years. To read more about the kings and queens of Great Britain, go to vgsbooks.com for links.

Henry VIII's daughter, Elizabeth I, became queen in 1558. The nation flourished under her rule. Explorers such as Sir Walter Raleigh and Sir Francis Drake explored the coasts of North and South America. Under Elizabeth I, Parliament gained more powers and was transformed from merely an advisory body to a decision-making group that was responsible for the writing and the passing of laws.

Meanwhile, Scotland remained a Catholic country. But this changed in 1560, when Elizabeth I helped Scottish Protestants take over the Scottish parliament. The Parliament named a Protestant as head of government while Mary—Margaret Tudor's granddaughter and heir to the Scottish throne—was being educated in France. Mary, Queen of Scots, returned to take over the throne the following year but, as a Catholic, she enjoyed little popular support from her Protestant subjects. In 1568 Protestant forces captured Mary and forced her to abdicate in favor of her son James. She fled to England, hoping to seek refuge with her distant cousin, Elizabeth I. Instead, Elizabeth imprisoned Mary in the Tower of London. But many English Protestants saw the Catholic Mary as a threat to Protestant England. And, in fact, Mary did become involved in some unsuccessful riots to unseat her cousin. In light of these actions, church and government leaders pressured Elizabeth I into executing Mary in 1587.

Elizabeth I never married and therefore had no heirs. As a result, she named Mary's Protestant son, James Stuart, her successor. Rather than unify the two countries, James chose to rule them separately. He ruled Scotland under the name of James VI. In England he ruled as James I. But unlike Elizabeth, James refused to share power with either parliament. When his son, Charles I, continued this policy, England again erupted into civil war. By 1642 the Royalists, who supported the

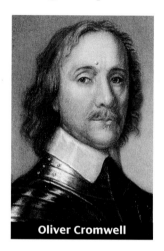

Oliver Cromwell

king, were pitted against the Parliamentarians, who supported Parliament. The latter, under the leadership of Oliver Cromwell, were victorious. Charles was tried and executed in 1649, and his heirs fled to France. Following Charles's execution, England became a republic, governed by Parliament. But in 1653, Cromwell disbanded Parliament, taking control of the country. Cromwell established illegal taxes, took away freedom of the press, and insisted that people follow his religious beliefs. After his death in 1658, England chose to reestablish the monarchy, offering the throne to Charles II, Protestant son of Charles I.

Charles II governed with the cooperation of a new Parliament. The Parliamentarians and the Royalists organized into political parties. The Whigs supported a strong Parliament at the expense of the monarch's power, while the Tories believed in a strong monarchy.

When Charles II died in 1685, his Catholic brother James II inherited the crown. Hostile to a Catholic ruling the country, Parliament removed him from the throne and offered it to James Stuart's Protestant daughter and son-in-law, Mary and William. They ruled jointly, within the confines of the Bill of Rights, a document that guaranteed freedom of speech and fair trials for English citizens.

The last of the Stuart monarchs was James II's youngest daughter Anne. In 1707 she signed the Act of Union that united England, Wales, and Scotland into the Kingdom of Great Britain. Under this act, all of Great Britain was to be governed by one Parliament in London, which consisted of representatives from all three countries. During this time, England competed with France for trade and territory in North America. England also competed with the Dutch and the Portuguese for markets in Asia through the British East India Company. This created more opportunities for trade of goods between Britain and other territories. As a result, a new class of wealthy merchants emerged.

Meanwhile in Ireland, disputes between Irish Catholics and English and Scottish Protestants led to increasing violence in the 1600s.

In 1692 Irish Protestants established an exclusively Protestant legislature. Protestants excluded Catholics from this parliament, the armed forces, and the legal profession. Catholics were also forbidden to buy land from Protestants or to carry arms. By the early eighteenth century, Irish Catholics owned only 5 percent of the land.

Expansion and Industrialization

Following the death of Queen Anne in 1714, the British crown passed into the hands of her German Protestant cousins of the House of Hanover. Under the Hanovarian dynasty, the monarchy gave up most of its authority to Parliament, which essentially governed the nation. Due to these expanded powers, Parliament required a single leader, called the prime minister, who worked with a group of officials called a cabinet to oversee various aspects of government. The monarchs came to have more of a ceremonial role.

The Hanovarian period also witnessed the expansion of land conquests in Asia, Africa, and the Americas. After a series of wars with France over ownership of eastern North America, the Treaty of Paris was signed in 1763. It gave France's North American colonies to the British, who governed them, as well as their own colonies along the Atlantic coast. Within a few years, burdensome taxes and other policies led some British colonists to call for independence. These actions led to the American Revolution (1775–1783), a long and bitter war between Britain and its American colonies. In 1783 the British admitted defeat, acknowledging the creation of the United States of America.

British soldiers (in red uniforms) fought a losing battle to crush the rebellion of Britain's thirteen American colonies during the American Revolution.

Britain maintained control of the former French colonies (part of present-day Canada).

On the domestic front, Great Britain united all of the British Isles under one rule when it officially made Ireland a part of the kingdom in 1801. The new union was named the United Kingdom of Great Britain and Ireland.

In the late eighteenth century, advances in mechanization moved the nation from a farm-based economy to an industrial economy based on manufacturing. This period came to be known as the Industrial Revolution. Working with new inventions such as weaving machines and power looms, British factories used raw materials imported from the colonies to create consumer goods such as fabric and clothing. At the same time, factories used coal in large quantities to fuel the new machines and factories. Urban work opportunities grew, and an increasing number of rural people found employment in factories in the cities.

Not only did the British workforce produce goods for its own population, but Britain also found markets for these goods within its own expanding empire. By the 1800s, British territorial possessions had grown to include Australia, New Zealand, India, Malaysia, and numerous other states in Asia, Africa, the Caribbean, and the South Pacific.

Yet not everyone benefited from this period of prosperity. While the owners of many manufacturing and import and export businesses became very wealthy, the speed of industrialization outpaced the cities' ability to provide proper housing for such an influx of people. As a result, most ordinary workers lived in cramped, unsafe conditions and worked in crowded, unsafe factories for low wages. Sickness and disease became rampant.

In response to cries for reform in the 1830s, the British Parliament began to regulate factory conditions, leading to safer, healthier environments for workers. Workers were allowed to form groups, called trade

POTATO FAMINE

In 1845 as many as 1 million people starved to death in Ireland when a blight (crop disease) destroyed its primary food source, potatoes. Several hundred thousand more Irish emigrated to Scotland, England, and North America. The British government's weak response to the famine led many Irish to question British rule. Some began to organize a movement to gain independence from Britain. They became known as Nationalists and founded an organization called Sinn Féin, meaning "we ourselves." However, citizens of Ulster, the majority of whom were Protestant, wished to maintain their ties with Britain. They came to be known as Unionists.

During the 1830s, unsafe **factory working conditions** caused the British government to create laws to protect workers.

unions, that could bargain with employers for better wages and working conditions. The right to vote was extended to some men. A new political party, called the Labour Party, was formed in 1900 to represent the interests and concerns of the working classes. Also in the late nineteenth century, a national education system was established, and some financial assistance was provided to the sick and elderly.

Empire and the World Wars

Meanwhile, Britain's colonial holdings continued to expand. In 1876 Queen Victoria declared herself empress of India, officially creating the British Empire. By the beginning of the twentieth century, the United Kingdom's economic and military might made it the most powerful empire in the world. Its colonies thrived on every continent except Antarctica. It was the most important center in the world for trading goods and borrowing and lending money.

But by this time, the nations of Europe were concerned about any one country dominating the others. These nations began to form competing alliances. The British formed an alliance with the French, the Russians, and others to rival the Central Powers of Germany, Austria-Hungary, and their supporters.

In 1914 the murder by a Serbian of the heir to Austria-Hungary's throne prompted an attack against the small eastern European country of Serbia. This action set in motion a series of events that led to war between the Central Powers and the Allies, as Britain's alliance was called. During World War I (1914–1918), millions of English, Scottish,

During **World War I, British troops** fire a machine gun while wearing gas masks to protect themselves from poison gas attacks.

Welsh, and Irish soldiers fought in Europe and the Middle East. Thousands of citizens from Britain's colonies joined in the war effort too. When the Central Powers finally surrendered in 1918, the British death toll was more than 800,000.

The war touched the lives of all British citizens. It blurred gender, race, class, and religious lines by forcing Britons to work side by side to defeat the enemy. When the war was over, the majority of people did not want to return to the remnants of the feudal society that had for centuries stressed class and gender lines. Women, who had received the right to vote in 1918, wanted to keep the privileges they had gained during the war by working at jobs that had previously been reserved for men.

The United Kingdom's post-World War I years were often characterized by internal strife and hardship. In 1920 the British Parliament passed the Government of Ireland Act, founding the Irish Free State. The six predominantly Protestant counties of Ulster in the north became a separate country, called Northern Ireland, which remained politically connected to the United Kingdom of Great Britain. Yet many Catholics in Northern Ireland did not want to live in a Protestant state. As a result, a group called the Irish Republican Army (IRA) began a campaign of harassment against the Protestants of Northern Ireland.

In the late 1920s, Britain was swept up in a global economic depression that lasted throughout most of the 1930s, leaving many Britons jobless and poverty-stricken. The effects of the depression were felt more sharply in the poorer regions of Scotland, Wales, and Ireland. This brought more cries for self-rule in these countries, because their citizens believed that the British government in London was not as concerned for the welfare of its non-English countries.

In 1931 the government of the United Kingdom passed the Statute of Westminster, acknowledging complete legislative autonomy (self-rule) for many of its former colonies and establishing the Commonwealth of Nations. The founding Commonwealth members were Canada, Australia, New Zealand, the Irish Free State, and South Africa.

Meanwhile, the aftermath of World War I had failed to solve Europe's many international disputes. By the late 1930s, Germany, under the leadership of Adolf Hitler, had become a military power and a threat to its neighbors. In September 1939, Germany invaded Britain's ally, Poland. Great Britain, France, and their allies responded by declaring war on Germany and its allies—known as the Axis Powers—sparking World War II (1939–1945). During the war, Britain and its allies fought in Europe, North Africa, Asia, and the Pacific.

During the early years of the war, German aircraft heavily bombed British cities. All the United Kingdom's major cities—including London, Liverpool, Hull, Bristol, Glasgow, Cardiff, and Belfast— suffered great damage. But despite this, Great Britain, led by Prime Minister Winston Churchill, refused to surrender. By 1942 the Allies had begun to

Winston Churchill *(second from left)* **and a group of advisors inspect bomb damage in London during World War II.**

push back Axis forces and by 1945 had forced Germany to surrender. Some 360,000 British soldiers died in the war.

The End of an Empire

World War II spelled the end of the British Empire. The nation lost 25 percent of its wealth as a result of the war, and the government could no longer support its overseas holdings, many of which were calling for independence. In the decade following the war, most of the colonies received their independence and joined the commonwealth.

Immediately after World War II, the Labour Party won a majority in Parliament and enacted generous social welfare legislation that provided basic social services, such as health, education, and retirement pensions to all citizens. The nation prospered during this period of postwar rebuilding, which also witnessed the nationalization (switch from private to government ownership) of major industries and services. Large government budgets—funded by higher taxes—helped to pay for the new services.

In 1949 the North Atlantic Treaty Organization (NATO) was formed among the United Kingdom, Canada, the United States, and various western European nations. NATO's main purpose was to create a counterbalance to the military threat of the Soviet Union and its Eastern European allies.

While Northern Ireland enjoyed economic growth in the immediate postwar period, the Catholic minority still lacked many civil rights enjoyed by Protestants. A peaceful civil rights movement began to correct

British troops were sent to quell violence in Northern Ireland during the late 1960s and 1970s.

this situation but was undermined by extremist groups on both sides. The worst period of violence, called "The Troubles," began in 1968 and continued throughout the 1970s.

The 1960s also saw the discovery of oil and natural gas deposits off the northeastern coast of Scotland. Since the 1970s, these reserves have helped the United Kingdom to become self-sufficient in oil and gas. Some of these products are also sold for export.

In 1973 the United Kingdom joined what would become the European Union, an economic union of European nations primarily designed to improve trade and cooperation among member nations. Not all Britons favored entry into the organization. While few dispute the financial benefits of free trade among EU nations, many are wary of being subject to the EU's laws and regulations—for example, immigration and environmental rules—and believe that membership has diminished some of Britain's independence.

In 1979 the Conservative (Tory) Party won a large majority under Britain's first female prime minister, Margaret Thatcher. To control government spending, which had risen greatly in the previous decades due to social welfare programs, Thatcher's government privatized (switched from state to private ownership) many state-owned enterprises, cut back social services, reduced the powers of labor unions, and greatly trimmed the size of the government.

After a long period of governments led by the Conservative Party, the Labour Party returned to power in the United Kingdom with the

Margaret Thatcher served as Britain's prime minister from 1979 to 1990, longer than any other British prime minister in the twentieth century.

election of Tony Blair as prime minister in 1997. Since then, he has concentrated on improving the nation's economy and bringing the United Kingdom into the twenty-first century with improved trade and political alliances.

Tony Blair

In Northern Ireland, a cease-fire between Protestant and Catholic militants was declared in 1997, and for the first time in twenty-five years, all sides sat down together to discuss peace. The Good Friday Agreement reached in 1998 states that the political future of Northern Ireland will be decided only by a majority decision within the country. A new assembly was formed that year, with all powers formerly held by the secretary of state for Northern Ireland turned over to the new assembly. But disagreements continued, and the Northern Ireland Assembly was finally suspended in early 2003.

Meanwhile, the longstanding calls for self-rule by Scotland and Wales were resolved in the late 1990s. In 1997 both Scotland and Wales produced majority votes in favor of "devolution," whereby governing powers would gradually be passed from London to legislatures in Edinburgh and Cardiff. The official transfer of powers to both countries took place on July 1, 1999.

Although no longer the world's foremost political and military power, the United Kingdom continues to wield its influence in international affairs and conflicts. During the late 1900s and early 2000s, the United Kingdom has been an active participant in global peacekeeping efforts. British troops were dispatched as peacekeepers in the former Yugoslavian republics of Bosnia and Herzegovina, and the United Kingdom participated in the NATO air offensive against Yugoslavia. The United Kingdom supported the U.S.-led offensive against international terrorists in Afghanistan and fought alongside U.S. forces in the war that deposed Iraqi leader Saddam Hussein. In 2004 several thousand British troops remain in Iraq, working to provide security to the country's citizens and to rebuild the troubled Middle Eastern nation.

Government

The United Kingdom is a constitutional monarchy governed by an elected Parliament. The reigning monarch is the symbolic head of state but holds no political power. Parliament consists of two houses. The House of Commons has 659 members who are elected by all citizens over the age of eighteen, in elections held no more than five years apart. The House of Lords is made up England's 24 top bishops (Anglican clergy); 92 of its hereditary peers (persons who have inherited their titles); the Law Lords (the country's highest-ranking judges); and people who were given seats in the house by the queen for outstanding public service under the Life Peerages Act of 1958. By 1999 the number of hereditary peers eligible to sit in the House of Lords had reached 750, but a law brought into effect that year reduced the hereditary seats to ninety-two. Although legislation may originate in either house, it is usually produced in the Commons. While the House of Lords may delay a piece of legislation or return it to the Commons with amendments or suggestions for improvement, it cannot prevent the bill from becoming law. A cabinet of ministers headed by the prime minister conducts the business of governing the nation and is responsible to the House of Commons.

Since devolution in 1999, Scotland and Wales each has its own elected parliament. In Scotland the assembly is comprised of 129 members, while the Welsh Assembly consists of 60 members. Each has the power to legislate on all domestic matters. In addition, the Scottish Assembly has the power to vary taxes set by the British Parliament by up to 3 percent. The Northern Ireland Assembly consists of 108 members and has the same authority over domestic matters as do Scotland and Wales. All three states also elect members to the British Parliament of the United Kingdom in London. Scotland elects 72 of the total of 659 members, while Wales elects 40, and Northern Ireland elects 18.

England, Wales, and Northern Ireland have judicial systems based on parliamentary legislation and common law. Serious offenses are tried in a crown court, before a judge and jury. Less serious offenses may be tried in magistrate courts or county courts.

Under the Act of Union between Scotland and England in 1707, Scotland has retained its own legal system. The Scottish system is based on Roman civil law rather than British common law. This means that legal decisions in Scotland are based on written laws from the past, while in the rest of the United Kingdom legal decisions are based on local customs and practices acceptable to the public at the time. Scotland's highest judicial officer, the lord advocate, tries all serious offenses in the High Court, while less serious offenses are tried by sheriff courts and district courts.

Visit vgsbooks.com if you'd like to learn more about the United Kingdom's constitutional monarchy, parliament, and its leaders.

THE PEOPLE

The United Kingdom has a total population of 58.8 million. Most Britons live in England, which has a population of 49.2 million. Scotland has the next largest population with 5 million people, while the population of Wales is 2.9 million. Northern Ireland is the smallest of the four countries, with a population of 1.7 million. The population of the United Kingdom has grown at a rate of 4.4 percent annually since 1981, primarily due to increasing birthrates and immigration.

Ethnicity

For centuries the indigenous people of the United Kingdom have shared a common ethnic ancestry. It was formed by a combination of invading peoples, including the Celts, Romans, Anglo-Saxons, Scandinavians, and Normans. Celtic influence is strongest in Scotland, Wales, and Northern Ireland, where it can be found in the language, music, and art. The predominant influences in England tend to be more Norman-French and Anglo-Saxon.

Over the centuries, the United Kingdom evolved a class system that distinguished between people of various classes of society. Originally, the distinctions were based on ownership of land. Those who owned land, usually the rich, were considered to be of one class, while those who did not belonged to the working class. These distinctions began to blur during the period of colonization as a new class of people who were profiting from trade began to emerge. In the twentieth century, as expanded voting rights allowed more citizens to vote, class distinctions became even less distinguishable. Social divisions still exist but are no longer as strict.

Following the rule of the Normans in the eleventh century, the United Kingdom experienced little foreign immigration. Not until the early part of the twentieth century did significant numbers of immigrants begin moving to the country. Most of these people were from continental Europe. They were followed in later decades by groups of immigrants from the British Commonwealth such as India, Pakistan,

People of Jamaican and African descent live mainly in Britain's urban areas.

Jamaica, and Hong Kong. Most of these immigrants settled in the large English conurbations such as London, Liverpool, Birmingham, and Bristol. Many live within larger communities of their own ethnic groups, where they feel a sense of belonging and expect to find jobs more easily.

This large influx of immigrants has strained the nation's educational, health, and social welfare systems, causing difficult economic conditions for all citizens. This course of events prompted the government to introduce the British Nationality Act in 1981, which placed severe restrictions on immigration and drastically reduced the number of immigrants.

Yet as a result of this mass migration from the commonwealth, the ethnic makeup of the country has changed during the past century. While most of Northern Ireland, Scotland, Wales, and northern and southwestern England are still populated primarily by descendants of the Celts and Anglo-Saxons, up to one-third of the population in the English conurbations is of nonwhite ancestry. That figure is expected to grow dramatically in the future due to higher birthrates among the nonwhite population and the continuing decline in the birthrate of the white population.

Fewer immigrants have made their homes in the United Kingdom's other countries. Although Scotland has a significant nonwhite community, Wales and Northern Ireland have far smaller numbers of immigrants.

Language

English is the official language of the United Kingdom. Yet, at one time, each country had its own separate language, some of which are still spoken in certain areas. The language of each country was influenced by the specific ethnic groups that occupied it. Therefore, the languages that developed in the four countries had many different roots.

English has its roots in the Germanic languages of the Anglo-Saxon invaders but was significantly changed with the addition of words from Norman French. By the late 1400s, a modern English was in use that had borrowed many words from other tongues. Modern English closely resembles this fifteenth-century form.

Each of the United Kingdom's many regions has a unique dialect. To English speakers outside these areas, these dialects—such as Cockney in London and Geordie in the north—can be difficult to understand.

While nearly all Scots speak English, a small percentage of those from the western Highlands and the Hebrides speak Gaelic as their primary language. Some residents of the Lowlands still speak Scots, a Scottish dialect used in Scottish literature, poetry, and song.

Of the three non-English countries, Wales has been most successful in maintaining its own language. A full 20 percent of Welsh citizens are able to speak Welsh Gaelic. Welsh, along with English, is an official language of Wales.

Only a small percentage of Northern Ireland's residents speak Irish Gaelic. Since the plantation period of the early seventeenth century, the English language became the dominant language of the country. In recent decades, Irish Gaelic is usually heard only in traditional poetry and song.

GAELIC

Gaelic was the language of the Goidelic Celts who settled in Northern Ireland and Scotland. (The Celtic peoples who settled in England and Wales were known as Brythonic Celts.) Original Gaelic had three forms: Irish Gaelic, Scottish Gaelic, and Manx. Irish Gaelic is the oldest of the three forms and dates back to the eighth century A.D. Manx became a separate dialect when speakers of Irish Gaelic were isolated on the Isle of Man. Finally, in the sixteenth century, Scottish Gaelic (which also contains Anglo-Saxon and Norse words) emerged as a distinct dialect. Few residents of the Isle of Man still speak Manx, and the language is nearly extinct.

Health and Social Services

The United Kingdom is a welfare state, meaning the government takes responsibility for the welfare of its citizens from birth to death. The state provides a minimum level of funding to meet the essential needs (such as food, shelter, and clothing) of all citizens who are unable to provide for themselves. Education, health, and social services are the sole responsibility of the state. The cost of health and social services makes up one of its largest expenditures at 6.9 percent of the gross domestic product (GDP), the total value of goods and services produced by a nation in a year.

All British mothers receive an allowance for every child, from birth to age sixteen, and up to age nineteen if the child continues to attend school. Single-parent families receive an additional allowance for their first child. Disabled persons, the elderly, and widows also receive allowances.

Under the National Insurance Scheme, all wage earners between the ages of sixteen and sixty (for women) and sixty-five (for men) pay into an employment insurance plan. In turn, the plan pays benefits to those who are unemployed, cannot work due to sickness or injury, or are of retirement age (sixty years for women and sixty-five years for men).

Under the National Health System (NHS), the government pays for most health care. Patients do not have to pay for hospitalization and consultations with doctors and other health care practitioners. Citizens are charged minimal fees for dental care, eye care, and prescription drugs. Although the system requires long waits for surgeries

In Britain, people of retirement age, such as this Scottish couple, are called **pensioners.** They receive regular income payments —called a pension— through Britain's National Insurance Scheme.

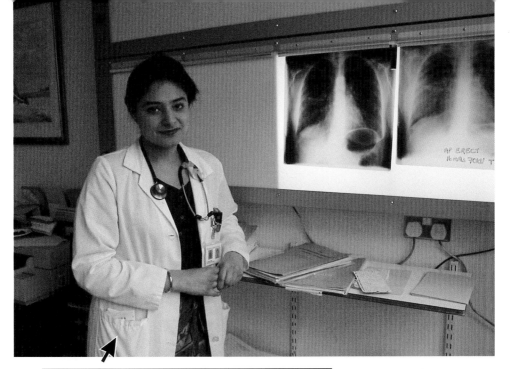

Most doctors work for the National Health System, although private clinics do exist in the United Kingdom.

and procedures for nonlife-threatening conditions, citizens of Britain agree that the benefits of the system far outweigh the problems. Its primary achievement is that Great Britain has one of the world's lowest infant mortality rates (5.4 deaths per 1,000 live births) and one of the world's highest life expectancies (78.2 years).

Government statistics show that about 49,000 Britons are infected with either the human immunodeficiency virus (HIV), or the disease caused by HIV, acquired immunodeficiency syndrome (AIDS). The National Health Service continues to work to educate the public about the dangers of HIV/AIDS and how to prevent infection and transmission of the disease.

▸ Education

Education from kindergarten through the university level is provided free of charge for students throughout the United Kingdom. The cost of public education is a major expenditure in the nation's budget, using up to 4.7 percent of the GDP.

School attendance is required for all children between the ages of five and sixteen in the United Kingdom, except for Northern Ireland, where education begins at age four. In England, Scotland, and Wales, children may also attend state-run or private nursery schools before the age of five. Children begin their education in primary school, after which most graduate to secondary school at the age of eleven. In many areas of England, children between the ages of eight and twelve or nine and thirteen attend middle school. Most secondary schools are known

Schoolchildren in Northern Ireland study in their small classroom. British schoolchildren receive an above average education compared to other nations, scoring fifth in reading, fourth in science, and eighth in math in a survey of thirty-two countries.

as comprehensive schools, and provide general education as well as college preparation and vocational training. They admit students regardless of academic abilities. Some grammar schools (which prepare students for college and university) only admit students who achieve high test scores. Most students complete their secondary education by age sixteen.

All state schools in England, Wales, and Northern Ireland have to conform to a national curriculum (study program), but in Scotland, the government only offers curriculum guidelines to its schools. In England some secondary schools are run under the Specialist Schools Programme, which allows schools to specialize in areas such as language, technology, arts, and sports, in addition to offering the regular state-authorized curriculum. The national curriculum provides for national testing of students at ages seven, eleven, and fourteen. At the end of secondary school, students take a national exam to qualify for the General Certificate of Secondary Education. At age eighteen, students wishing to go on to postsecondary education take examinations in a few selected subjects in order to receive a General Certificate of Education, Advanced Level. Since 1989 many students also take Advanced

Supplementary examinations and obtain a higher standing in a broader range of subjects.

Following secondary school, students may further their education at universities or polytechnics (technical schools that grant degrees in fields such as engineering, architecture, and computer studies). Most postsecondary undergraduate degree programs are three to four years long. There are 47 universities in England, 12 in Scotland, one in Wales, and two in Northern Ireland. England and Wales together have 35 polytechnic universities, Scotland has five, and Northern Ireland two. Although university education is paid for by the state in state-run universities, seats in these institutions are very limited and, therefore, available only to students of the highest academic standing.

In 1971 the United Kingdom launched the Open University, a university with no physical campus. The institution, created to make higher education accessible to more citizens, conducts classes with the use of television, radio, correspondence, and summer schools and grants degrees as other universities do. Although common these days, the idea was unique and advanced for its time.

Students at the University of Cambridge, in Cambridge, England, attend a chemistry lecture. Cambridge is one of the oldest universities in the world.

CULTURAL LIFE

Although members of a single nation that shares many common aspects of history and geography, England, Scotland, Wales, and Northern Ireland have maintained distinct cultural identities. In particular, Scotland, Wales, and Northern Ireland have worked hard to maintain their unique cultural traditions in spite of their long history of living under English rule.

▷ Religion

In the post-World War II years, religion has played a diminishing role in the lives of many citizens of the United Kingdom. Important religious festivals such as Christmas, Easter, Yom Kippur, and Ramadan are still celebrated, yet regular attendance of services during other times of the year has seen a marked decline. Across all denominations, adult attendance of religious services has declined from 10.2 percent in 1980 to 7.7 percent in 2000.

The government census of 2001 found 72 percent of the English population was Christian, 6 percent belonged to other faiths, 14

percent claimed to have no religion, and 8 percent did not state their religion.

Among Christian faiths, the Church of England, the official religion of England, has the largest number of members. Its 27 million members are known as Anglicans. The Roman Catholic denomination is the next largest, with 4 million members. Protestant sects, known as free churches, are the Baptist, the Methodist, and the United Reformed Church.

England also has approximately 325,000 members of the Jewish faith, making it one of the largest Jewish congregations in Europe. Religions of the country's newer immigrants, such as Islam, Hinduism, and Buddhism, are also present in England.

In Scotland, the official religion is the Protestant Church of Scotland, which counts some 2 million members. The Roman Catholic Church is next in size, followed by smaller groups of Protestant denominations and non-Christian religions.

During the United Kingdom's 2001 census, 390,000 people in England and Wales listed their religion as Jedi, the fictional belief system of the Star Wars movies. The unusual tally was the result of a widely circulated e-mail hoax, which stated that if 10,000 people listed Jedi as their religion, the government would put Jedi on its list of official religions.

The Church of Wales is the predominant Protestant church in Wales and is similar to the Anglican Church in its beliefs and practices. Methodists form the next largest group, while Catholics only have a small presence in Wales. In Northern Ireland, Protestants outnumber Catholics by about 3 to 1. The distribution of Protestants to Roman Catholics across the country is quite uneven, though, with one group often outnumbering the other in any given rural or urban area.

Literature, Music, and the Arts

The United Kingdom has a long and rich literary tradition that has impacted the world. One of the earliest English writers was the eighth-century historian known as the Venerable Bede, who wrote *Historia Ecclesiastica*, a religious history of the English people, in Latin. Wales has one of the oldest literary traditions in Europe, which can be traced back to the sixth-century folktales and legends preserved in *The Mabinogion.* Fourteenth-century English writer Geoffrey Chaucer wrote *The Canterbury Tales.* Many literary scholars consider this book of stories to be the finest work written in Middle English. William Shakespeare, the best known and most read writer in the English language, wrote his plays and poetry between 1564 and 1616. His works include *Hamlet, Macbeth, Romeo and Juliet,* and *King Lear.*

In the late eighteenth and early nineteenth centuries, William Blake, William Wordsworth, Lord Byron, and Percy Shelley carved for themselves important positions in literary history with their poetry. Although written in poetic terms, their works addressed important social issues of the period. This period also produced many women writers, the best known among them being Mary Shelley *(Frankenstein),* Jane Austen *(Pride and Prejudice, Emma)* and the Brontë sisters: Charlotte *(Jane Eyre),* Emily *(Wuthering Heights),* and Anne *(Agnes Grey).*

Robert Burns, whose short life spanned only thirty-seven years in the late 1700s, was Scotland's most famous literary figure. By the age of twenty-seven, he was already considered "The Bard of Scotland." He wrote in the Scots language and greatly helped to keep the language alive by encouraging people to read it. In the same century, noted literary figure Adam Smith, also a Scot, wrote *The Wealth of Nations,* an important work of economic theory. Another Scottish writer of this period, Sir Walter Scott, was noted for his historic novels such as *Rob Roy* and *Ivanhoe.*

Charles Dickens is perhaps the most famous English novelist. In his writings, such as *Oliver Twist* and *A Christmas Carol,* he portrayed the social problems of the 1800s. His depictions of the impoverished working class increased public awareness of their difficulties and brought about important social changes in Britain. Equally important, although in the world of science, was his contemporary, Sir Charles Darwin *(The Origin of Species),* who wrote about his research into the science of human evolution. The popular adventure novels of Scottish writer Robert Louis Stevenson *(Kidnapped* and *Treasure Island)* were penned during the nineteenth century, as was his famous short story *The Strange Case of Dr. Jekyll and Mr. Hyde.* And the fictional detective, Sherlock Holmes, was created by another Scot, Sir Arthur Conan Doyle.

The English literary tradition continued to grow throughout the twentieth century, with more works about the social situations of the times. Noted writers include novelists Virginia Woolf *(To the Lighthouse)* and William Golding *(The Lord of the Flies),* and the playwright Noël Coward *(Private Lives).* Detective novels by Agatha Christie *(The Mousetrap)* found great popularity, as did the fantasy novels of J. R. R. Tolkien (The Lord of the Rings Trilogy*).* Popular children's writers include A. A. Milne *(Winnie the Pooh),* Beatrix Potter *(The Tale of Peter Rabbit),* and J. K. Rowling (the Harry Potter books).

The twentieth century also produced the best-known literary figure from Northern Ireland. C. S. Lewis *(The Chronicles of Narnia),* a native of Belfast, was a prolific novelist, poet, essayist, literary critic, and scholar. Northern Ireland has had a very long tradition of poets, among them Seamus Heaney *(Death of a Naturalist)* of Londonderry, who won the Nobel Prize for Literature in 1995. Perhaps the most famous Welsh writer of modern times was Dylan Thomas, who wrote in the mid-1900s. In his poetry, as well as his play *Under Milk Wood,* he chronicled the lives of ordinary Welsh people. Thomas's contemporary, Richard Llewellyn, wrote *How Green Was My Valley,* a story of a Welsh mining town.

C.S. Lewis

The United Kingdom also has a rich musical tradition. As far back as the sixteenth and seventeenth centuries, composers such as Thomas

Tallis and William Byrd were noted for their church music. Henry Purcell was one of the eighteenth century's most popular musicians. During the late nineteenth century, Sir William Gilbert and Sir Arthur Sullivan wrote several popular operettas. In the twentieth century, many artists such as Benjamin Britten, Sir Edward Elgar, Gustav Holst, and Ralph Vaughan Williams have composed new music, as well as revived old English folk songs.

Great Britain has been a hotbed of popular music since the 1960s, when acts such as the Beatles, the Rolling Stones, and Pink Floyd created a global demand for British music. In the 1970s, performers such as Elton John and Eric Clapton achieved worldwide fame.

Meanwhile, British acts influenced new musical trends such as heavy metal (Motorhead, Black Sabbath, featuring Ozzy Osbourne) and punk rock (the Sex Pistols, the Clash). In the 1980s, groups such as the Smiths, the Cure, and Duran Duran enjoyed great popularity. The 1990s saw the rise of a new genre of music called Britpop, in which many

The Beatles *(clockwise from left, Ringo Starr, Paul McCartney, John Lennon, and George Harrison)* are perhaps the most popular rock and roll act in history. All four band members grew up in Liverpool, England.

Britpop group **Blur** has enjoyed worldwide popularity since the mid-1990s. Frontman Damon Albarn *(above)* is also a member of the multinational experimental rap group Gorillaz.

British groups, including Blur, Radiohead, the Verve, the Spice Girls, and Super Furry Animals, created rock music with a distinctly British flavor.

Theater, Television, and Film

The United Kingdom is one of the world's major theater centers. In the twenty-first century, some fifty theaters operate in London's West End theater district, producing both new and historical plays. The Royal Shakespeare Company in Stratford-upon-Avon and the Globe Theatre in London present the famous playwright's plays.

The United Kingdom also has a vibrant movie industry and has produced some of the world's foremost filmmakers, including the "master of suspense" Sir Alfred Hitchcock, director of *Vertigo* (1958), *Psycho* (1960), *The Birds* (1963), and many other popular films. Other acclaimed filmmakers include Sir David Lean, who directed the epics *Lawrence of Arabia* (1962) and *Dr. Zhivago* (1965), among others, and Ridley Scott, director of *Gladiator* (2000) and *Black Hawk Down* (2001). Other popular British films include the long-running James Bond series and the Harry Potter films.

Television is also a very important part of British culture, and British viewers have a variety of channels to choose from. Programming features a wide variety of news, sports, comedy, movies, game shows, soap operas, and reality TV. *Coronation Street*, a soap opera, is one of the

The cast and crew of **Coronation Street** gather in the show's pub, Rovers Return, for a Christmas photo.

country's most popular programs and has been on the air for more than forty years.

Two of the most watched are the British Broadcasting Company's channels, BBC 1 and BBC 2. These networks have no commercials, and every Briton who owns a television has to pay for a license, which helps to fund the programming. British cable viewers have access to a number of North American networks, including MTV, Nickelodeon, and Cartoon Network.

Festivals and Holidays

As a nation made up largely of Christians, Christmas is the most widely celebrated festival in the United Kingdom. Traditional British family celebrations include special meals and the arrival of Father Christmas bearing gifts. Among non-Christian faiths, the most important religious celebrations are Yom Kippur, the Jewish Day of Atonement that usually falls in September or October, and the festival that follows Ramadan, the Muslim holy month.

For many Scots, Hogmanay (New Years' Day) surpasses Christmas in importance. Burns Night, which honors the birthday of the great Scottish poet, is celebrated on January 25 with the ceremonial dish, haggis, and the recitation of Burns's poem "Address to a Haggis." In Wales, St. David's Day is celebrated on March 1, during which people adorn their lapels with symbols of Wales, such as a miniature red dragon or a leek (an onionlike vegetable). In Northern Ireland, the Protestants celebrate Orangeman's Day on July 12, the date the Protestant William of Orange defeated the Catholic King James II of England at the Battle of the Boyne in 1690. Catholics celebrate St. Patrick's Day on March 17 by wearing a green shamrock—the emblem of St. Patrick.

Hogmanay, from the Gaelic word for "new morning," is what the Scots call New Year's Day. Edinburgh hosts a large street party for more than 10,000 people. The ancient custom of "first footing," where the first person to enter a house after midnight (preferably a tall, dark man) is expected to bring a gift is still practiced faithfully. Women and red-headed visitors are considered bad luck, as are visitors not bearing gifts.

Many important cultural festivals take place throughout the United Kingdom. One such festival is the Royal National Eisteddfod (Welsh for "a session"), the primary venue for celebrating traditional

Celebrants in traditional costumes dance during the **Royal National Eisteddfod.**

Welsh culture. At this weeklong event, held each August, musicians, singers, dancers, writers, poets, and visual artists showcase their talents through competitions and performances. In Scotland the Edinburgh International Festival is a major celebration of the arts, as well as a show of military skills during the Military Tattoo. The bagpipe, the signature instrument of Scotland, is always heard at Highland gatherings, accompanying the traditional dances and marches.

◉ Sports and Recreation

The United Kingdom is a nation of sports lovers. Team sports in particular are a very important part of daily life. Football (soccer) is the nation's most popular sport. Played by young and old alike, it is also the nation's primary spectator sport. Manchester United, the United Kingdom's top team, has dominated national competition in recent years. Cricket, a game similar to baseball, is also very popular. Many Britons also enjoy rugby, a rough and fast-moving

Rugby is typically played without protective gear. Many players sustain serious injuries on the field.

game with similarities to American football. Rugby is especially popular in Wales. Tennis has a celebrated tradition in Britain, and the annual Wimbledon tournament—held every June—is professional tennis's most prestigious event. Badminton and horseback riding are also popular sports in the United Kingdom, while snooker (a type of billiards) is a very popular indoor game.

The game of golf was invented in Scotland and is played on courses throughout the United Kingdom. The Highland Games, a collection of popular traditional sports played during Scotland's annual clan gatherings, include tossing the caber (a huge, heavy log), putting the shot, and throwing the hammer.

A straining Scot prepares to **toss the caber.** A caber may weigh as much as 150 pounds (68 kilograms) and be as long as 18 feet (5.5 meters). Some historians think that this sport was developed by lumberjacks to help them practice throwing tree trunks into the river. For links where you can find out more about the United Kingdom's rich cultures, traditions, literature, music, dance, current events, cuisine, and much more, go to vgsbooks.com.

▶ Food

The traditional diet of the United Kingdom varies in each of the four countries according to tradition and the availability of ingredients. Because Scotland and Wales have farmland that is better suited to live-stock, their consumption of meats (lamb, bacon) is high. England and Northern Ireland have more access to vegetables, in particular root crops (turnips, carrots, parsnips, and potatoes) and cole crops (cabbage, brussels sprouts, and broccoli). England is also renowned for its fine cheeses, including cheddar, from the village of Cheddar in southwestern England, and Stilton, from the district of the same name in east-central England. As an island nation, seafood has always been a mainstay of the United Kingdom, although much of its ocean species have been depleted. In recent decades, the influx of immigrants from the former British colonies has exposed the British palate to more spicy foods from the Indian subcontinent, the West Indies, Asia, and Africa.

Traditional culinary favorites include fish and chips (fries); beef and kidney pie; shepherd's pie, a casserole of seasoned ground beef topped with mashed potatoes; roast beef and Yorkshire pudding; bangers and mash (sausages and mashed potatoes); and Cornish pasties, turnovers filled with meat, spices, and potatoes. In Scotland, haggis is a staple both at ordinary meals and celebrations. This Scottish delicacy is made of a sheep's stomach lining stuffed with a mixture of the animal's internal organs, oatmeal, and spices. Staple soups include Scotch broth, with beef or lamb and vegetables, and cock-a-leekie, with chicken and vegetables. Kippered (brined and smoked) herrings are the most popular fish.

In Wales, cawl, a thin broth with bacon and vegetables, is a popular one-dish meal, as is Welsh rarebit, which consists of thick slices of bread

Yorkshire pudding *(top center)* is a soft, puffed pastry baked in meat drippings. In a traditional **English Sunday lunch** featuring roast beef, Yorkshire pudding, mash (mashed potatoes), and cooked vegetables are served before the meat is brought to the table.

SHEPHERD'S PIE

Shepherd's pie, a classic Scottish dish, remains a popular staple food in the United Kingdom. It is traditionally served at supper, the evening meal that usually consists of a main course and dessert. In Scotland, shepherd's pie is often prepared using lamb, but this recipe uses ground beef.

3 large potatoes, peeled and halved

2 tbsp. margarine or butter

salt and pepper to taste

¼ c. milk

1 tbsp. vegetable oil

1 large onion, chopped

1 lb. lean ground beef

1 large carrot, peeled and grated

½ tsp. dried thyme

1 tbsp. chopped fresh parsley

½ clove garlic, peeled and finely chopped, or pinch of garlic powder

1 tbsp. soy sauce

1. Cook potatoes in 2 quarts boiling salted water until soft (about 15 to 20 minutes).
2. Drain off water and add margarine or butter, salt, and pepper. Mash potatoes, adding enough milk to make a smooth mixture. Set aside.
3. Preheat oven to 375° F.
4. Heat oil in a large skillet and sauté onion until soft. Stir in ground beef, and then add carrot, thyme, parsley, garlic, salt, and pepper. (Don't use too much salt because soy sauce is salty.) Cook for another 5 minutes. Add soy sauce and stir well.
5. Spread meat mixture in a deep pie dish. Spread mashed potatoes evenly over meat mixture and swirl with a fork to create an attractive pattern.
6. Bake the pie on the middle rack of the oven for 30 minutes, or until top is lightly browned. Serve immediately.

covered with melted cheese. Northern Irish traditional foods are very similar, with Irish broth being the traditional soup, and colcannon—cabbage and mashed potatoes flavored with chives and sometimes, bits of bacon—a popular staple. The Irish also enjoy biscuits made with baking soda known as soda bread and other types of whole grain breads.

Tea from its former Asian colonies has been a British staple for the past three centuries, making the United Kingdom the sixth-largest tea consumer in the world. Coffee is also a popular beverage. British lagers and ales are traditionally the most popular alcoholic drink in the United Kingdom, although some people enjoy Irish and Scotch whiskey.

THE ECONOMY

Although no longer the hub of the world's largest and most power-ful economic empire, the United Kingdom remains one of the world's top financial powers. With a GDP of $1.4 billion, the United Kingdom has the world's fourth-largest economy, with major holdings in the banking, insurance, manufacturing, and shipping industries.

In 1973 the United Kingdom joined the European Economic Community (later the European Union, or EU), an organization of European countries that has removed most barriers to the movement of goods, workers, capital, and services among member nations. Britain's involvement with the EU remains a divisive issue. While membership has had some positive effects, most notably opening the European market to British goods, many Britons oppose being subject to the EU's laws and regulations regarding immigration, fiscal policy, and the environment.

◉ Manufacturing and Trade

Since the Industrial Revolution of the nineteenth century, the United Kingdom has remained heavily dependent on manufacturing and on the export of its manufactured goods. Manufacturing, which includes oil, natural gas, and mining, contributes 25 percent of the GDP and employs 25 percent of the workforce, making the United Kingdom the world's sixth-largest manufacturing nation. Central and southern England and the Central Lowlands of Scotland are dotted with manufacturing plants that produce everything from ships, aircraft, locomotives, automobiles, and electronic equipment, to textiles and food. Scotland produces 50 percent of all the complex electronic equipment used in the United Kingdom, as well as 20 percent of the computers used in EU countries.

The manufacturing of iron and steel products is concentrated in northeastern England and southern Wales, near the region's iron and coal deposits. The textile industry still plays a large role in the

For centuries, **British sheep** have produced some of the world's most prized wools.

economies of Scotland and Northern Ireland. Yarn, rope, and carpets of jute are still produced there, although the raw materials have to be imported. In Northern Ireland, Belfast is the production center for linens, while the majority of clothing manufacturing takes place in Londonderry. The United Kingdom is the world's seventh-largest producer of wool. The fine woolen yarns and fabrics made from prized Hebridean and Shetland sheep's wool form a very important part of Scotland's export industry. Scotch and Irish whiskey play important roles in the exports of Scotland and Northern Ireland, respectively. Wales, with its excellent deepwater port facilities, has become one of the most important oil ports in the United Kingdom, with huge plants that refine crude oil in preparation for export. Most of Northern Ireland's exports are to the other three countries of the United Kingdom, and most of its imports are from these countries as well.

Most of the United Kingdom's exports are manufactured products—fuels and food products. Despite the nation's high performance in manufacturing, it still imports more manufactured goods than it exports, primarily food, beverages, and tobacco. Great Britain's chief trading partners are the United States, Germany, France, and the Netherlands.

The discovery of large deposits of oil and natural gas off the northeastern coast of Scotland in the 1960s and 1970s provided a major boost to the United Kingdom's economy, while making the nation self-sufficient in the two commodities. The nation produces the world's fourth-largest output of natural gas and the tenth-largest

An oil rig in Cromarty Firth in northeastern Scotland

supply of oil. In total energy output, the United Kingdom ranks sixth in the world.

Southern Wales and northern England once were the hubs of an enormous coal and iron mining industry. Although some of the country's coal mines are still worked, many are no longer in use. Reasons for this change lie in the move away from coal to cleaner-burning fuels such as natural gas, hydropower, and nuclear energy. Scotland, with its many mountains and rivers, contains the largest hydropower facilities in the United Kingdom, supplying all of its own electricity needs, as well as those of northern England. Small amounts of limestone, slate, and gold are mined in Wales.

Transportation, Tourism, and Services

During the 1970s, the United Kingdom experienced a major movement of people from urban inner-city areas to suburban communities. This caused a rapid growth in automobile ownership. At the same time, domestic freight transportation switched from rail to road. All these factors placed enormous

The Channel Tunnel, or Chunnel for short, is an enormous tunnel that crosses beneath the English Channel between Shakespeare Cliff, near Dover, England, and Sangatte, France. At just over 31 miles (50 km), it is the second-longest railway tunnel in the world and carries high-speed trains across the channel in about thirty-five minutes. The tunnel, which opened in 1994, carries approximately half the passenger and freight traffic between England and France.

demands on the highway network throughout the kingdom. Consequently, major financial investments have been made to the nation's 231,102 miles (371,913 km) of highways. In addition, the United Kingdom maintains an efficient railway commuter service, with 10,564 miles (17,000 km) of track. All large cities have their own inner-city transportation systems, some of which include underground railway systems. The London Underground subway system, dubbed "the Tube," is one of the world's longest.

Eight airports serve both international and domestic air traffic. Heathrow, Gatwick, and Stansted are located near London. Heathrow is the world's fourth-busiest airport, serving some 60.7 million passengers per year, including the highest number of international passengers annually. London, Liverpool, Hull, Milford Haven, Glasgow, and Belfast are the major cargo ports, while Southampton, Dover, Belfast, and Glasgow are important passenger ports.

As the world's sixth most popular tourism destination in the world, the United Kingdom attracts 29.2 million tourists annually. This makes the nation the fifth-largest tourism revenue earner in the

Tourists gather in front of Buckingham Palace, the royal family's London residence.

world, with receipts of more than $23 billion per year. The nation's history and pageantry associated with a reigning monarch are attractions to many tourists. Visitors flock to the many castles and great houses throughout England, Scotland, and Wales; enjoy the cultural venues in the various capitals; and travel to quaint villages throughout the nation.

Services are the fastest-growing sector of the United Kingdom's economy, making up 73 percent of the GDP and employing 74 percent of the workforce. Community, government, and personal services (such as health care, education, legal services, and military operations) make up the largest segment of the service sector. The trade, hotels, and restaurants segment is next in importance, followed by tourism. Finance, insurance, real estate, and business services (banking, insuring homes and cars, buying and selling houses, advertising, and accounting and tax services) make up the next largest segment. Finally, transportation and communication (all forms of travel and the media) also receive revenue from the tourism industry.

Agriculture

Agriculture contributes only 2 percent of the GDP and employs only 1 percent of the United Kingdom's workforce. Western England has pastureland and supports large dairy and beef industries. Sheep are raised mostly in northern England and throughout Scotland. In Scotland, farmers raise dairy cattle in the southwestern lowlands and beef cattle in the northeastern lowlands. Most vegetable crops and potatoes are grown in the Fens, while the south and southeast produce fruit crops, sugar beets, and grains such as wheat and barley. In Wales, sheep are raised in the higher central

POUNDS AND PENCE

The United Kingdom's earliest form of currency, the penny, was minted in the sixth century and was named for King Penda of Mercia (ruler of a kingdom in west-central England). It was the only coin in existence in the United Kingdom until the thirteenth century. At that time, 240 pennies were equal in value to one pound of silver. Eventually, a system of pounds (£), shillings (s), and pence (d) evolved. Under that system, 1£=20s, and 1s=12d. In addition to these denominations, there were also the guinea (21s), the crown (5s), the half-crown (2.5s), the sixpence, the three-penny (called a thr'penny), the half-penny (called a ha'penny), and the quarter-penny (called a farthing). The complicated system was changed in 1971, when 100 pence came to equal one pound. Convert U.S. dollars to British pounds at vgsbooks.com.

MAD COW DISEASE

In early 1996, the United Kingdom's cattle industry was devastated by an epidemic of bovine spongiform encephalopathy (BSE, or mad cow disease), a degenerative brain disease that not only kills cows (*above*), but can cause a deadly illness in humans who consume infected meat. As a result, the European Union immediately banned all British beef in EU countries, further crippling the British beef industry. The industry was just recovering from the devastating effects of the incident when, in winter 2001, it was struck by hoof-and-mouth disease, another infectious disease caused by a virus that attacks hooved animals. Once again, the European Union imposed a ban on British beef. More than two million head of cattle and sheep had to be slaughtered before the virus was brought under control.

moors, while cattle are raised on the coastal lowlands and inland valleys where pasture, hay, and other feed crops such as barley and oats grow.

◉ The Future

The future holds many challenges for the United Kingdom, both as a single nation, and as four distinct countries within that nation. A key issue facing both citizens and leaders is the country's role within the European Union. While Britons enjoy the economic benefits brought by free trade with its continental neighbors, a large percentage of British citizens have misgivings about allowing the EU to influence or control the country's monetary, trade, and immigration policies.

A similar issue of identity concerns two of the countries within the nation, Scotland and Wales. Despite being part of Britain for three centuries, in recent decades both countries have become preoccupied with the threat of losing their individuality within the United Kingdom. The subsequent devolution of government to the two states in 1999 was a much-celebrated event.

Northern Ireland faces a distinct challenge of its own. The national government and Northern Irish citizens are working to find a democratic solution that would satisfy the rights and needs of both the Protestant majority and the Catholic minority. The majority of the Northern Irish population favor the devolution of governing powers to the Northern Ireland assembly. Yet a vocal minority of both Protestants and Catholics object to the process.

Another key issue among Britons is the future of the country's monarchy. The British royal family no longer serves any significant role in ruling the country. Because of this, some citizens have questioned whether the monarchy should be abolished to save taxpayer money. Britons are also having difficulty reconciling their historic vision of a ceremonial, formal, and dignified monarchy with a royal family that desires increasingly to act as ordinary British citizens.

Yet these are not impossible challenges for a nation with such a successful and tenacious history. Solutions will be found, as they have been in the past, in the desire of its citizens to propel their great nation into yet another millennium.

In 2002 **Queen Elizabeth II** celebrated fifty years on the throne with a Jubilee Tour of the country. At Wells, school children waved British flags to welcome her.

Timeline

ca. 24,000 B.C.	Skeletal remains from Paviland Caves in southern Wales have proven that human habitation existed there during this period.
6000–5000 B.C.	Melting ice submerges land bridge between Britain and mainland.
ca. 500 B.C.	A warlike people from north-central Europe known as Celts invade the British Isles.
A.D. 43	Romans conquer Britain and establish Londinium (London).
ca. 400s	Britain is invaded by Angles and Saxons from northern Europe.
793	The first Viking invasion of Britain takes place.
c. 1000s	Brian Boru unifies all of Ireland and is crowned king of Ireland. Gruffydd ap Llwelyn unifies Wales. Scotti king Duncan I unifies all Scotti lands into one kingdom, Scotland.
1066	Normans from France invade and conquer England, and William I (the Conqueror) becomes the first Norman king of England.
1154	William's grandson, Henry II, becomes the first Plantagenet king.
1215	King John signs the Magna Carta.
1328	England accepts Scotland's declaration of independence and recognizes Robert the Bruce as King Robert I.
1337	Edward III claims the French throne and begins the Hundred Years' War with France.
1485	Henry VII ascends the throne and establishes the House of Tudor.
1534	Henry VIII breaks with the Roman Catholic Church and forms the Church of England.
1536	Wales is united with England.
1547	Edward VI begins the "plantation" of Ireland during which Protestants from England move into Catholic Ireland.
1560	Elizabeth I assists John Knox in taking over Scottish parliament.
1649	Charles I is executed, and England becomes a republic headed by Oliver Cromwell.
1660	The English monarchy is reestablished, as Charles II ascends the throne with limited royal powers.
1707	Queen Anne signs the Act of Union, uniting England, Wales, and Scotland into the Kingdom of Great Britain.

1714   The British crown passes to the German house of Hanover, under George I.

1776   Great Britain's American colonies declare independence, and the United States of America is formed.

1783   The British government accepts defeat in the American Revolution, signing the Treaty of Paris, which officially recognizes the United States of America as an independent nation.

1800s   The Industrial Revolution begins in Great Britain.

1801   Ireland is united with Britain to form the United Kingdom of Great Britain and Ireland.

1845   A potato blight leads to a massive famine in Ireland, during which about 1 million Irish die.

1900   The Labour Party is formed as a means of providing a voice to the nation's working class.

1914-1918   British forces fight in World War I.

1920   The Government of Ireland Act calls for the division of Ireland into Northern Ireland (which remains politically connected to Britain) and the Irish Free State.

1931   The Statute of Westminster acknowledges complete autonomy of Great Britain's dominions and establishes the Commonwealth of Nations.

1939-1945   British forces fight in World War II.

1949   Great Britain becomes a charter member of the North Atlantic Treaty Organization (NATO).

1968   "The Troubles," a period of increased violence between Catholics and Protestants, begins in Northern Ireland.

1973   Great Britain joins the European Economic Community (later the European Union).

1982   Argentine forces invade the British-administered Falkland Islands. British forces drive them out during the Falklands War.

1997   The Labour Party is voted the ruling party of the United Kingdom. Labour's leader, Tony Blair, becomes prime minister.

1998   A new Northern Ireland assembly is elected.

1999   Independent assemblies are elected in Scotland and Wales.

2001   Great Britain supports the U.S.-led offensive against international terrorists in Afghanistan.

2003   British forces, as part of an international coalition led by the United States, invade Iraq and depose Saddam Hussein.

COUNTRY NAME The United Kingdom of Great Britain and Northern Ireland

AREA 94,214 square miles (244,014 sq. km)

MAIN LANDFORMS The island of Great Britain, the northern part of the island of Ireland, the Shetland Islands, the Orkney Islands, the Inner and Outer Hebrides, the English Lowlands (England), the Fens (England), the Highlands (Scotland), the Central Lowlands (Scotland), the Southern Uplands (Scotland)

HIGHEST POINT Ben Nevis, 4,406 feet (1,343 m) above sea level

LOWEST POINT The Fens, 13 feet (4 m) below sea level

MAJOR RIVERS Thames, Severn, Tay, Clyde, Dee, Upper and Lower Bann, Erne

ANIMALS Deer, foxes, stoats, weasels, badgers, otters, moles, shrews, hedgehogs, rabbits, brown hares, rats, mice, squirrels, toads, frogs

CAPITAL CITY London

OTHER MAJOR CITIES Birmingham, Leeds, Liverpool, Manchester, Edinburgh, Glasgow, Cardiff, Belfast, Londonderry

OFFICIAL LANGUAGE English

MONETARY UNIT British pound. 1£ = 100 pence.

BRITISH CURRENCY

The monetary unit of the United Kingdom is the British pound, represented by the symbol "£." One hundred pence (p) make 1£. Notes are printed in denominations of £1, £5, £10, £20, and £50. Coins represent denominations of £1, £2, 50p, 20p, 10p, 5p, 2p, and 1p.

The official flag of the United Kingdom, the Union Flag, is often called the Union Jack. Its origins date back to when James VI of Scotland inherited the English throne in 1603. Since England and Scotland had separate flags, confusion existed regarding which flag James's ships should fly at sea. So he ordered the creation of a new flag that superimposed the English red cross of Saint George on the Scottish white cross of Saint Andrew. When Ireland was added to the kingdom in 1801, the red cross of Saint Patrick was added.

The national anthem of the United Kingdom is "God Save the Queen." It was originally performed in 1745 as "God Save the King," but the word "king" throughout the anthem is changed to "queen" whenever the reigning monarch is female. It was officially adopted as the national anthem in the early nineteenth century. It has three stanzas, the first two of which are printed below.

"God Save the Queen"
God save our gracious queen
Long live our noble queen
God save the queen!
Send her victorious,
Happy and glorious,
Long to reign over us;
God save the queen!

Oh! Lord our God arise,
Scatter her enemies
And make them fall.
Confound their politics,
Frustrate their knavish tricks,
On Thee our hopes we fix,
Oh! Save us all!

 For a link where you can listen to the United Kingdom's national anthem, "God Save the Queen," go to vgsbooks.com.

GERRY ADAMS (b. 1948) Adams, the leader of Sinn Féin, a Northern Irish political party that supports unification with the Republic of Ireland, was born in West Belfast. During the 1970s, he was arrested and imprisoned many times for violent activities. He was elected as a member of the British House of Commons from 1982 to 1992 but never took his seat. He has been president of Sinn Féin since 1993.

DAVID BECKHAM (b. 1975) British soccer sensation David Beckham was born in London. Growing up, he became a loyal fan of Manchester United, the top British football team. As an eighteen-year-old his dream of playing for his favorite boyhood team came true, and he soon became the team's top midfielder, playing on the team for ten years. In 2003 he was traded to Spain's Real Madrid team for $41 million.

KENNETH BRANAGH (b. 1960) Born in Belfast, Branagh has had a varied film career as an actor and director. He has acted in many of the films that he also directed, including *Henry V* (1989), *Dead Again* (1991), *Peter's Friends* (1992), and *Much Ado about Nothing* (1993). In 1996 he wrote the screenplay for, acted in, and directed the film *Hamlet*.

SIR WINSTON CHURCHILL (1874–1965) Born to an English statesman (Lord Randolph Churchill) and an American heiress (Jennie Jerome) in Oxfordshire, England, Churchill was prime minister during much of World War II, from 1940 to 1945. His strong-willed leadership helped the country play a major role in the defeat of the Axis Powers by the Allies. Also a brilliant writer of history and biography, he received the Nobel Prize for Literature in 1953.

SIR SEAN CONNERY (b. 1930) Born and raised in Edinburgh, the handsome, dark-haired Connery is one of the world's most popular and recognizable actors. His most famous role was as the original James Bond, the British secret agent. He appeared as that character in seven films, including *Dr. No* (1962), *From Russia with Love* (1963), and *Goldfinger* (1964). Since that time, Connery has gone on to appear in dozens of other popular films, including *The Untouchables* (1987), *Indiana Jones and the Last Crusade* (1989), *The Rock* (1996), *Finding Forrester* (2001), and *The League of Extraordinary Gentlemen* (2003).

SAINT DAVID (ca. 520–ca. 600) Saint David, the patron saint of Wales, was born near Saint Bride's Bay, in Pembrokeshire, Wales. He was one of several missionaries who traveled around Wales in the sixth century, spreading Christianity. He founded a religious community in Mynyw in southwestern Wales, where he followed a frugal lifestyle, living only on bread, water, and herbs. His final words were said to have been, "Be cheerful and keep your faith." There are over fifty churches in Wales dedicated to the saint, and his feast is celebrated annually throughout Wales on March 1.

DIANA, PRINCESS OF WALES (1961–1997) Born in Sandringham, Norfolk, Diana Spencer was a nineteen-year-old kindergarten teacher when she married Prince Charles, heir to the British throne, in 1981. She and the prince were divorced in 1996, and she died in a car accident in Paris in 1997. Thousands of people still flock to her burial site on the Spencer family estate near Northampton in the Midlands.

DAVID LLOYD GEORGE (1863–1945) Raised in a small village in northern Wales, David Lloyd George served as prime minister of the United Kingdom during the final two years of World War I. He headed the Liberal government of Britain between 1916 and 1922 and was the instigator of the early foundations of the modern British welfare state.

SIR ISAAC NEWTON (1642–1727) Born in Woolsthorpe, Lincolnshire in eastern England, Newton was one of the world's greatest scientists. He made landmark contributions to the fields of physics, mathematics, and astronomy. His theory of gravity explained how the universe is held together. His discoveries in optics explained how white light is a mixture of all colors. Newton also invented a new kind of mathematics—calculus.

SIR WALTER RALEIGH (ca. 1554–1618) Born in Devonshire in southeastern England, Raleigh was an adventurer and writer. He was a close associate of Queen Elizabeth I and used his connections to amass a great deal of wealth and property. In the late 1500s, he sponsored or led a series of expeditions to North and South America. These included the establishment of a short-lived colony on the island of Roanoke, off the coast of Virginia. Raleigh also published accounts of many of his adventures. Imprisoned several times for angering first Queen Elizabeth and her successor, James I, Raleigh was executed in 1618.

J. K. ROWLING (b. 1965) Author of the Harry Potter books, Joanne Kathleen Rowling was born in Chipping Sodbury, Gloucestershire, in southwestern England. Rowling first studied to become a secretary, but preferred to dream up stories rather than type up notes for her boss. She later developed her famous character, the wizard Harry Potter, while teaching English in Portugal. Each title in the Harry Potter series has sold tens of millions of copies, and the books have been made into a series of successful movies.

QUEEN VICTORIA (1819–1901) Born at Kensington Palace, London, Victoria assumed the throne at the age of eighteen and was Britain's longest-reigning monarch. Under Victoria's rule, Britain acquired numerous colonial territories across the world. In 1876 Victoria was proclaimed empress of India, officially creating the British Empire. At the same time, Victoria also allowed the monarchy a diminishing role in political affairs, gradually ceding control of power to elected officials during her reign.

BUCKINGHAM PALACE Located at the end of The Mall in the Saint James neighborhood of London, Buckingham Palace is the official residence of the reigning British monarch. The original building belonged to the Duke and Duchess of Buckingham. It first became a royal residence in 1762, when King George III and Queen Charlotte lived there. It has since been redesigned and renovated many times. The palace is open to the public during July and August, when the royal family is on its summer vacation.

GIANT'S CAUSEWAY This famous geological attraction is located on the northern coast of Northern Ireland in County Antrim. The collection of thirty-eight thousand hexagonal basalt columns was formed by a volcanic eruption that forced lava into fissures in the existing chalk beds. Eventually, the chalk was eroded by the ocean, exposing the collection of columns. More colorful local folklore credits the Celtic giant Fionn MacCumhail with building the causeway to a nearby Scottish island.

GLOBE THEATER Completed in 1997, the Globe Theater in London is an exact replica of the venue in which Shakespeare acted and presented many of his plays between 1599 and 1613. The original burned down in 1613. The new theater is built of green oak and willow, with a thatched roof and plaster walls.

THE ROYAL MILE This route in Edinburgh connects Edinburgh Castle (Scotland's official royal residence) to Holyrood, an alternate royal residence. Studded with historic buildings—such as Saint Giles Cathedral, Tron Kirk, and John Knox's House—this is easily the most historic mile in Scotland.

STONEHENGE The most impressive and famous of the historic stone circles that exist throughout the British Isles, Stonehenge is truly one of the world's mysteries. Construction is believed to have begun around 3000 B.C., with further building taking place between 2100–1900 B.C. and then again in 150 B.C. Because the stone circles point to sunrise in midsummer and sunset in midwinter, they are believed to have religious significance involving the cycles of the sun. But it still remains a mystery how the primitive people of these times were able to transport these giant rocks from the Atlantic coast of Wales. Stonehenge is located on Salisbury Plain, about 80 miles (128 km) southwest of London.

TOWER OF LONDON Located on Tower Hill on the north bank of the Thames River, the Tower of London dates back to the eleventh century. Its most notorious role is that of a prison for royalty and nobles awaiting execution during the Tudor reign. It is the home of the crown jewels—the magnificent collection of jewel-studded crowns, swords, and scepters (ceremonial batons) used by centuries of British royalty.

conurbation: a large populated region surrounding a city, whose economy is centered on that city. A conurbation includes the city and its suburbs.

devolution: the transfer of powers from the British parliament to the independent parliaments of Wales, Scotland, and Northern Ireland, permitting them to govern themselves.

European Union: an organization of European countries that promotes cooperation among its members in matters of politics and economics

Gaelic: the language of the Celtic people who invaded Britain in 500 B.C. and who lived there for many centuries before becoming integrated with the Anglo-Saxons. Gaelic is still spoken by some Britons.

gentry: the richer classes of people in the United Kingdom, most of whom have inherited lands from their ancestors

glen: a narrow valley

gross domestic product (GDP): a measure of the total value of goods and services produced within a country in a certain amount of time (usually one year). A similar measurement is gross national product (GNP). GDP and GNP are often measured in terms of purchasing power parity (PPP). PPP converts values to international dollars, making it possible to compare how much similar goods and services cost to the residents of different countries.

henge: a circular formation of stones of varying sizes, made by Stone Age and Bronze Age people of Britain, believed by archaeologists to be of religious significance

missionary: a person who travels to various parts of the world to spread a particular religion

moor: a gently rolling land made up of chalk, covered with short grasses, shrubs, and other low-growing plants. Moors are not suited for agriculture, except for grazing livestock.

privatization: the practice of changing a business or industry from public to private ownership

Protestantism: the general name for hundreds of non-Catholic Christian sects and denominations, including the Church of England. First developed in Germany in the 1500s, Protestantism denies the universal authority of the pope, considers the Bible the only source of revealed truth, and regards faith in God's grace as one of its key principles.

serf: a landless person who works for the rich classes, in return for food, shelter, clothing, and protection

Glossary

Black, Jeremy. *The Making of Modern Britain*. Phoenix Mill, UK: Sutton Publishing Ltd., 2001.
This book is a good survey of the progression of British history, economy, and social affairs from the beginning of the industrial revolution in the late eighteenth century to the end of the twentieth century.

Central Intelligence Agency (CIA). 2003.
<http://www.cia.gov/cia/publications/factbook/geos/uk.html> (October 28, 2003)
The World Factbook section of the CIA's website contains basic information on the United Kingdom's geography, people, economy, government, communications, transportation, military, and other issues.

Darby, John, ed. *Northern Ireland: The Background to the Conflict*. Belfast, UK: Apple Tree Press, 1983.
This is an account of "The Troubles" of modern Northern Ireland and the history that led to the conflict.

Davies, Norman. *The Isles: A History*. New York: Oxford University Press, 1999.
This hefty volume, written by a well-known British historian, covers the history of Great Britain and Ireland from the prehistoric age to the 2000s.

Duffy, Seán. *The Illustrated History of Ireland*. New York: Contemporary Books, 2000.
The author provides a comprehensive account of Irish history from its beginnings as a single country, through the events of partition, to the present reality of two separate countries.

The Economist. 2003.
<http://economist.com> (October 28, 2003)
The Economist's website contains articles on the current economic, political, and social situation of the United Kingdom.

The Europa World Yearbook 2002. London: Europa Publications Limited, 2002.
This annual publication contains a detailed survey of the United Kingdom, including post-World War II history, government, economic affairs, social welfare, education, the constitution, ministries and their current incumbents, political organizations, and judicial system.

MacLean, Fitzroy. *Scotland: A Concise History*. New York: Thames and Hudson, 2000.
Filled with vivid photos, this book provides a concise history of Scotland from the prehistoric age through the 1990s.

McKittrick, David. *Endgame: The Search for Peace in Northern Ireland*. Belfast, UK: The Blackstaff Press, 1995.
This book is an account of the Northern Ireland conflict, as written by a correspondent for the British newspaper *The Independent*, who covered the breaking news stories at the height of the conflict during the 1970s and 1980s.

Selected Bibliography

O'Connor, Fionnuala. *In Search of a State: Catholics of Northern Ireland.* Belfast, UK: The Blackstaff Press, 1993.
Through firsthand accounts from both Catholic and Protestant men and women of varying ages and occupations, the author shows the effects of the Catholic/Protestant conflict in Northern Ireland.

Population Reference Bureau. 2003.
<http://www.prb.org> (October 28, 2003)
The annually updated statistics on this site provide an excellent source of demographic information for the United Kingdom and other countries, on everything from birthrates and death rates, to infant mortality rate, and percentage of the population with HIV/AIDS.

Schama, Simon. *A History of Britain: Volume 1: At the Edge of the World: 3000 B.C.–A.D. 1603.* New York: Miramax Books, 2000.
The first volume in Simon Schama's three-part companion series to the television miniseries *A History of Britain* covers Britain's history from the prehistoric age to the end of Queen Elizabeth I's reign.

————. *A History of Britain: Volume 2: The Wars of the British: 1603–1776.* New York: Miramax Books, 2001.
Filled with stunning photos, volume 2 of the History of Britain series covers the nation's rise as a world power.

————. *A History of Britain: Volume 3: The Fate of Empire: 1776–2000.* New York: Miramax Books, 2002.
The third volume in the History of Britain series follows the rise and fall of the British Empire, covering events from the American Revolution to 2000.

Strong, Roy. *The Story of Britain.* New York: Fromm International Publishing Corporation, 1996.
Written by one of Britain's foremost historians, Sir Roy Strong, this book provides a strong narrative of Britain's history.

Thompson, Wayne C., and Mark A. Mullin. *Western Europe 2000: The United Kingdom.* Harpers Ferry, WV: Stryker-Post Publications, 2000.
The authors provide a concise, current economic, political, and social survey of the United Kingdom, from an American perspective.

Austen, Jane. *Pride and Prejudice.* **New York: Bantam, 1983.**
First published in 1813, Austen's amusing comedy follows the spirited courtship between Elizabeth Bennet and Mr. Darcy.

BBCi (British Broadcasting Corporation Interactive). **2003.**
Website: <http://www.bbc.co.uk> (October 28, 2003)
The website of the British Broadcasting Corporation has information on British culture, current affairs, and a wealth of information on the history of all four countries, including a test-your-knowledge game about British monarchs.

Brontë, Emily. *Wuthering Heights.* **New York, Penguin Classics, 2002.**
Emily Brontë's haunting tale of the love between Heathcliff and Catherine Earnshaw is a classic of English literature.

Carpenter, Angelica Shirley. *Lewis Carroll: Through the Looking Glass.* **Minneapolis: Lerner Publications Company, 2003.**
Learn more about the interesting life of Charles Dodgson, who wrote *Alice's Adventures in Wonderland* and *Through the Looking Glass* under the pen name Lewis Carroll.

Collins, David R. *J. R. R. Tolkien: Master of Fantasy.* **Minneapolis: Lerner Publications Company, 1992.**
This book follows the long and fascinating life of J.R.R. Tolkien, author of *The Hobbit* and the Lord of the Rings Trilogy.

Dickens, Charles. *Great Expectations.* **New York: Barnes and Noble Books, 2003.`**
One of Dickens's most popular novels, *Great Expectations* follows the rags to riches story of Phillip Pirrup, otherwise known as Pip.

Dommermuth-Costa, Carol. *William Shakespeare.* **Minneapolis: Lerner Publications Company, 2002.**
Read about the fascinating and mysterious life of the brilliant playwright and poet William Shakespeare.

Donovan, Sandy. *The Channel Tunnel.* **Minneapolis: Lerner Publications Company, 2003.**
This title in the Great Building Feats series follows the building of the great tunnel beneath the English Channel that links Great Britain and France.

Farman, John. *Short and Bloody Histories.* **Minneapolis: Lerner Publications Company, 2000.**
Written by a British author with a distinctly British sense of humor, the books in the Short and Bloody Histories series—*Knights, Highwaymen, Pirates, Ghosts,* and *Spies*—provide entertaining history lessons in these high-interest topics.

Havelin, Kate. *Queen Elizabeth I.* **Minneapolis: Lerner Publications Company, 2002.**
This is a biography of Elizabeth I, who reigned as queen of England for forty-four years.

Further Reading and Websites

Hill, Barbara W. *Cooking the English Way.* Minneapolis: Lerner Publications Company, 2003.
Find out more about English cooking, English food traditions, and make your own popular English dishes with this volume of the Easy Menu Ethnic Cookbook series.

Krohn, Katherine. *Princess Diana.* Minneapolis: Lerner Publications Company, 1999.
Learn about the extraordinary life and tragic death of Diana, Princess of Wales, one of the United Kingdom's most popular figures.

Roberts, Jeremy. *The Beatles.* Minneapolis: Lerner Publications Company, 2002.
This biography covers the lives and careers of John Lennon, Paul McCartney, George Harrison, and Ringo Starr, the wildly popular British pop music quartet of the 1960s.

————. *King Arthur.* Minneapolis: Lerner Publications Company, 2001.
This volume in the How History Is Invented series examines the life and times of both the historical and legendary Arthur.

Ruth, Amy. *Jane Austen.* Minneapolis: Lerner Publications Company, 2001.
This is a biography of the popular English author, who wrote such celebrated works as *Pride and Prejudice, Sense and Sensibility,* and *Emma.*

Smith Kenyon, Karen. *The Brontë Family: Passionate Literary Geniuses.* Minneapolis: Lerner Publications Company, 2003.
This is a biography of the Brontë sisters, Charlotte, Emily, and Anne, who wrote such English literary classics as *Jane Eyre, Wuthering Heights,* and *Agnes Grey.*

Toht, Betony, and David Toht. *Daily Life in Ancient and Modern London.* Minneapolis: Runestone Press, 2001.
This volume in the Cities through Time series explores the London of past and present with colorful illustrations and fascinating text.

Turk, Ruth. *Charlie Chaplin: Genius of the Silent Screen.* Minneapolis: Lerner Publications Company, 2000.
This is a biography of the great English-born movie actor and director, who went on to superstardom in Hollywood in the early 1900s.

vgsbooks.com
Website: <http://www.vgsbooks.com>
Visit vgsbooks.com, the home page of the Visual Geography Series®, which is updated regularly. You can get linked to all sorts of useful online information, including geographical, historical, demographic, cultural, and economic websites. The vgsbooks.com site is a great resource for late-breaking news and statistics.

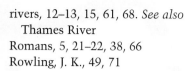

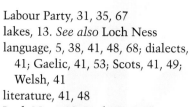

Captions for photos appearing on cover and chapter openers:

Cover: London's Tower Bridge has straddled the Thames River since 1894 and is one of the most recognizable bridges in the world.

pp. 4–5 Leeds Castle, a Norman castle built on two islands in a lake in central England, was originally built as a royal manor in A.D. 857. From 1278 onward, it was used as a royal palace by King Edward I.

pp. 8–9 Perched on England's southeastern coast, the White Cliffs of Dover overlook the English Channel, a narrow body of water that separates Britain from mainland Europe.

pp. 20–21 Stonehenge, an ancient stone monument in southwestern England, was erected in several stages from 2800 to 1800 B.C. It may have been designed to observe astronomical events such as eclipses.

pp. 38–39 Welsh girls dress in traditional costumes and wave Welsh flags to celebrate Saint David's Day, a Welsh holiday.

pp. 46–47 Royal guards stand at attention during a celebration called Trooping the Colour. This event takes place every summer in London in celebration of the queen's birthday. It involves a long parade of royal troops past the queen, royal family, and British public.

Photo Acknowledgments

The images in this book are used with the permission of: © TRIP/G. Pritchard, pp. 4–5; Digital Cartographics, pp. 6, 10; © Ric Ergenbright/CORBIS, pp. 8–9; © Eugene Schulz, pp. 11, 12, 13, 16–17, 56, 60; © TRIP/M. Stevenson, pp. 15, 54; © TRIP/C. Hamilton, p. 18; © TRIP/H. Rogers, pp. 19, 40, 43, 68; © Erin Liddell/Independent Picture Service, pp. 20–21; © The Pierpont Morgan Library/Art Resource NY, p. 23; © Erich Lessing/Art Resource, NY, pp. 24–25; © Bettmann/CORBIS, pp. 26, 28, 49, 50; © Archivo Iconografico, S.A./CORBIS, p. 27; Library of Congress, pp. 29, 31; © Hulton-Deutsch Collection/CORBIS, pp. 32, 34; By Trustees of the Imperial War Museum, p. 33; © TRIP/A. Pleavin, p. 35; AP/Wide World Photos, p. 36; Tim Graham/CORBIS, pp. 38–39, 65; © Bo Zaunders/CORBIS, p. 42; © Peter Turnley/CORBIS, p. 44; © Patrick Ward/CORBIS, p. 45; © TRIP/Adina Tovy, pp. 46–47; © STEFF/CORBIS KIPA, p. 51; © Granada Television, 1995, p. 52; © Ted Spiegel/CORBIS, p. 53; © TRIP/S. Grant, p. 55; © TRIP/J. Robertson, p. 61; © TRIP/B. Turner, p. 62; © TRIP/M. Peters, p. 64.

Cover photo: © TRIP/I. Corse. Back cover photo: NASA.